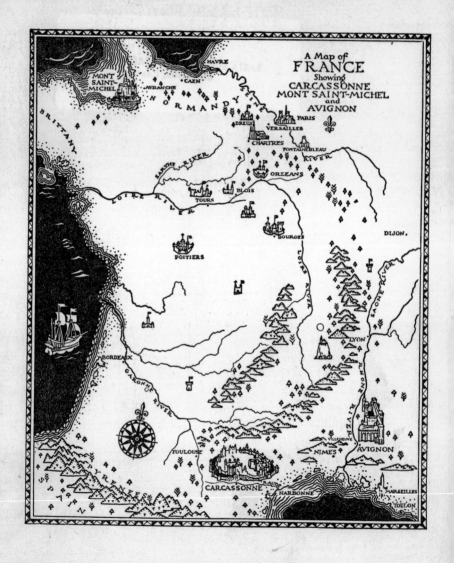

BEHIND
THE BATTLEMENTS

Text by
GERTRUDE LINNELL

Pictures by
HELENE CARTER

THE MACMILLAN COMPANY
N E W Y O R K   1931

PRINTED IN THE UNITED STATES OF AMERICA
BY THE STRATFORD PRESS, INC., NEW YORK

TO

PETER

AND THE TWINS

JOAN AND JANE

CONTENTS

CHAPTER   PAGE

I. CARCASSONNE: THE BATTLEMENTS OF THE BAR-
BARIANS

 1. "The Peace of Allah" 1

 2. Living Behind the Battlements . . . 28

II. AVIGNON: THE BATTLEMENTS OF THE POPES

 1. "Realm and Empire!" 63

 2. Popes and Nobles 92

III. MONT SAINT-MICHEL: THE BATTLEMENTS OF
THE MONKS

 1. Accolade 117

 2. A City in the Sea 145

CARCASSONNE

THE BATTLEMENTS OF THE BARBARIANS

THE CHRISTIANITY OF THE HEBREWS.

"The Peace of Allah"

EURIC toiled boldly up from the river toward the high battlements of the city he called Carcasona. Even in that day, when every city was surrounded by a high wall, Carcassonne was a wonder to all eyes. It stood so nobly on the hill, and its ancient Roman walls were so thick and long and many-towered. Euric loved it. It was home to him, though he had not seen it for two years. His heart beat faster as he thought that very soon now it would be home again, in reality.

Until he reached the city gates Euric knew that he was safe enough, but at the gates stood a strong Arab guard, with more inside the tower, ready in case of need. Euric's light hair and gray eyes marked him for a Christian among the dark Arabs. They might let him through. There were many Christian boys in the city, boys who had not felt that duty called them to fight. If they did not recognize him he would pass through

1

with the others. If they did recognize him he would be thrown into prison, perhaps killed as a traitor. He had gone to the Court of Aquitaine and to the army of Pepin, though he had been born and lived for fifteen years under Arab rule. To

EURIC·TOILED·BOLDLY·UP·FROM·THE·RIVER·TOWARD·CARCASONA

them he was a traitor. He was fighting for the man who had united France to drive the Arabs back across the Pyrenees.

Now, as he climbed he prayed. He prayed in Latin, of course, for Latin was the language of the Church, and in Euric's time it was believed also to be the language of God.

You could pray to the saints in other languages, but not to God. It would be taking a liberty with the majesty of God to speak to him in a language understood by common people.

"*Pater noster,*" Euric prayed, "*qui es in coelis, sanctificetur nomen tuum . . .*" And then, as he saw the turbans of the Arab soldiers almost beside him, "Oh, holy St. Martin, intercede for me, let me enter—" He did not know how to say all that in Latin. He could say only two prayers in Latin, and he had very little idea what they meant. If the saint would be merciful to him he might pass, and he must pass!

The sun was hot, he had been walking since dawn; he was tired and longed to rest in the cool shade of the narrow streets. But first there were the soldiers. Slowly he repeated the Arab salutation, "The peace of Allah be upon you!" He took care to walk almost in the center of the group of people. There were an old woman and two girls and a boy or so carrying water from the river and fagots. There were Arab ladies wearing long veils of bright colors, walking always two or three together; there were old men, and Arab soldiers. All Arab men were either priests or soldiers. You could tell Arabs in the dark from Christians, because they smelt cleaner, and used perfumes of sandalwood or musk. Euric liked the perfumes and their cleanly ways. The Count's men-at-arms sometimes laughed at him; they were inclined to think cleanliness unnecessary, if not actually sacrilegious. But Euric's mother was part Gaul and part Roman, tall with reddish hair, and as clean as the Arabs. She had taught him to be clean too.

"The peace of Allah be upon you!" he said loudly as he came abreast of the soldiers at the gate. "The peace of Allah be upon you!"

Before him was an old woman bent under the weight of a bundle of fagots, beside him a young girl carrying two heavy pails of water, behind him walked an old man who carried nothing. They were all Christians, and stood aside politely to let two stately Arab women pass. Their heavy silver jewelry jingled as they walked. It took courage to stand quietly within reach of the tall guards' curved swords while those two women walked slowly through the gates, but it must be done. If he had not waited he would have been scolded by the guards, for he was a Christian, and the Arabs forced the Christians to humility before their conquerors.

But the guards said nothing, and with murmured thanks to St. Martin, Euric found himself inside the great wall, in the grateful shade of the two huge towers that guarded the gateway. He was home again, after two years among the Count's men-at-arms. Home! He had not known how much he loved all the different people about him, the reddish-haired Gauls, the broad, yellow-haired Goths, the noble-nosed Romans, and even the thin, brown-faced enemy Arabs. This was home, and the Arabs had made the city cleaner and more orderly than the cities of Francia and Burgundy. They owned slim, beautiful horses, too. Euric had almost forgotten the noble grace of the Arab horses.

He went swiftly on into the heart of the town, finding his way among the narrow twisting streets, noting that one house had a new window beside the door, another a new carved grating, and that a bad hole in the street had been paved over since he had last been there. He had not known that the picture of the streets was so clearly etched on his brain. He turned a sharp corner and narrowly missed colliding with a noble Arab lady and her two black maids, all thickly veiled. He murmured humbly, eyes cast down, "The peace of Allah be upon you!" and ran. He was almost home. The greatest danger that remained was that one of his Christian neighbors might shout his name in careless surprise. If some one should call the attention of the Arabs to a boy who had for two years been at the Court of Aquitaine with the Count, and was now in the army of Pepin! "St. Martin, oh, St. Martin!" he murmured over and over, in supplication.

Then he was standing·before the door of that tiny, cool house where he had been born, and where he had lived all of his childhood. The Arabs, of course, had taken possession of the large house of his grandfather. Euric had never known its comfort, though his mother liked to speak of the days when she had been rich.

He was knocking, and footsteps were sounding behind the great oaken door—his mother's footsteps. He felt hot tears fall on his hand. He was home again, and his mother was coming to the door to let him in. "St. Martin, St. Martin!" he breathed, and then, for fear lest the great Lady Virgin should feel neglected, he prayed again, *"Ave Maria, gratia plena—"*

Mirela, his mother, was standing in the doorway. Euric pushed past her quickly and shut the door behind him. They stood in the shadow together. She spoke, and her voice was quick with fear. "Who are you?" she asked.

"Euric, your son." He was surprised. He had no idea that it would be possible for her not to know him. He would have known her anywhere, but then he realized that he had grown

THE SOLDIERS OF EURIC'S DAY DRESSED THIS WAY.

in two years, grown taller and heavier, and had learned the ways of the men-at-arms, the swagger and rougher speech of the North.

"Euric!" she cried, and drew him into the light from two small windows. She held him at arm's length and stared. "Euric indeed," she said, gravely, "and since I am a woman I must cry to see you here, my son—but do not be mistaken. I cry for happiness and the joy of seeing you. How tall you are, and like a man already!"

"It is two years," he answered.

"Two years," she repeated, slowly. "You have been a joy and a pride to my heart for seventeen years."

Euric laughed suddenly. "You were always one to count, like the priests," he said. "When I went to the court I found that it is outlandish to count the years of your age. No one does it except priests and a few women, and some of the Arabs. It is not manly to count the years of your age."

"The Romans," Mirela answered, "were the greatest conquerors in all the world and yet very learned. They knew much more than the years of their ages, so you see it may not be the fashion to count and read and write, but it is certainly not unmanly."

"It is old-fashioned, then," Euric said stoutly, "and I should hate to have my friends among the Count's men-at-arms know that I knew the number of years I had lived. They would laugh."

"Then we will not tell them until you are old enough and big enough so that they will not dare to laugh," said Mirela, smiling. Euric thought about that for a moment, but he could think of no answer that seemed good enough, so he changed the subject.

"My father sent me with greetings and a message," he said. "He would not dare to come himself."

"He would send you where he would not dare to come himself?" she asked, angry.

"You do not understand, my mother," said Euric. "He could not come. He would be known at once for a stranger, for he has been away so long that he does not know the Arab ways. They would question him and know him then for a captain of the Count's, and the Count is the Duke's man, and the Duke has joined the army of Pepin."

"I know that," said Mirela. "It means there will be war."

"Yes," said Euric, proudly. "I know my way here, and the Arab greetings, and I have changed so much they would not know me. Even you did not know me at first. It was quite safe for me to come. My father is brave—you should know that. If he had not been brave he would have stayed here to live quietly under the Arabs."

"True," said Mirela. "I am sorry I spoke so quickly. It is long since I have seen your father, Son, almost ten years. He may have changed greatly in that time—must have changed. In the days of the Romans there was peace in all the land of Gaul. That was the golden age. But now the land is full of armies tearing husbands from wives and sons from mothers, burning farms and bridges and cities, and stealing cattle and grain."

"Fighting is a man's business," said Euric.

His mother laughed. "There are better businesses for men than fighting," she said. "Perhaps there will come a time when all the nations of Gaul and Germania will give fealty to the Frankish king, and make an end to fighting."

"If you knew the army of Pepin you would not say that," Euric answered. "The Frankish king is nothing. Pepin is

king in all but title. And his men must fight some one. While
men are brave they will always fight."

"May God teach them peace!" said Mirela.

"That," said Euric, "is treason. You must not talk like
that before the soldiers when they come."

THE FRANKISH KING.

"When they come?" Mirela's voice caught him sharply.

"Yes, that is my message. They are coming here. You
have time, to-morrow early, to come away with me, and seek
shelter to the north. My father and I found a place, a warm,
dry cave on a hillside above the river. It is easy to reach and
sheltered, and a small stream runs near it. You could stay
there with one or two friends for a year and be safe."

"Hiding in caves," she scorned, "like an animal!"

"This is war," said Euric. "You cannot stay here, and clean and learned women do not travel with the army. It would be different if my father were a great captain or a noble. He is but a captain of men-at-arms. Yet even the wife of a noble could not be more safe than in the cave we chose. The siege here may be a year in length. There will be hunger and thirst for those who stay, and street fighting and pillage after we conquer. The Arabs may kill all the Christians within the city, for fear of betrayal. Come with me to-morrow, Mother."

"No," said Mirela.

"Why not?" Euric asked, surprised.

"I stay," said Mirela, stoutly. "I have my own bravery, Euric. I will not hide in a cave on a mountain. I can endure the hardships of a siege, and take my chances if the city falls, but the Arabs will not kill me, and I will not betray them. They have been kindly overlords, I have many friends among them, and this is my home. I stay."

"My father orders you to leave," said Euric. "He is your husband. You must obey him."

"I will obey him," said Mirela, smiling, "when he tells me himself to leave. While he is afraid to come he cannot send me orders, even by you, my son."

Euric started to answer hotly, but stopped as he heard a knock on the outer door. "Do not go," he cautioned. "If they find me they will kill me."

"I must go," she said. "If I do not they will know that I have something here to hide, then they will surely kill us both. Get into the bed and pull the curtain across it. Lie still and you will be safer than if I do not open the door."

Euric walked around the fireplace in the center of the room, to the bed in the wall. It was like a cupboard with a rough woolen curtain before it that could be drawn on cords. He jumped in, and lay down gratefully on the soft skins spread smoothly across oak boards. Then he pulled the curtain, and waited, silent, stretching out to rest his tired body. Mirela opened the door, and a veiled Arab woman entered with her black maid. She spoke as soon as the door was shut behind her.

"I have called you friend, Mirela," she said, "and I come to you as a friend, trusting you to do me no harm."

"Why should I harm my friend, Fathma?" Mirela asked. The Arab lady pushed back her blue cotton veil and stood looking gravely at Mirela.

"Because your son is here," she answered, "and you will be afraid. We have a saying that he who is afraid is more dangerous than he who fears not."

"That is true," said Mirela.

"I saw your son," said Fathma. "He passed me in the street, and I knew him, though he is changed since he went away. He has served the enemies of the Prophet. Is it as our enemy that he is here?"

Euric pushed aside the woolen curtain, and stepped out

into the room. "It is a long while," he said, swaggering a little, "since I have heard the name of the Prophet. I had almost forgotten that you call yourselves followers of the Prophet, but I had not forgotten, Hanum, that you have sons who were my friends. I should like to see them again. Ali was always trying to do the things Achmed and I did, and when he hurt himself he never cried."

"He is grown tall now," said Fathma, "almost as tall as you, and he is very skillful with the scimitar, and can recite much of the Koran without help from his teacher."

"And can he read and write?" Euric asked a little scornfully.

"Oh, yes," Fathma answered, proudly.

"Well, I can't," Euric announced.

"Once you could," Fathma was surprised. "Once you used to show me your wax tablets and the Latin words written evenly on them. You hated to have them melted off again to write more."

"I forgot that when I went among the Count's men-at-arms," said Euric. "Reading and writing are for priests and women, not for fighting men."

"The Gothic and Frankish fighting men drove out the Romans," Fathma said sternly. "If you drive us out also, the land of the Gauls will have known a thousand years of peaceless darkness before such brightness as the Romans knew shall be again. So says the imam. We came to offer you the salvation of Islam. If you refuse it Allah will punish you."

"We choose the salvation of Christ," said Euric.

"Jesus of Nazareth was a great prophet and a learned man," said Fathma gently, "but the savage peoples who fight under the Frankish banners do not follow his teachings. They are barbarians, dressed in skins, coarse and ignorant. Leave them, Euric, while there is yet time. Save yourself

EURIC WROTE ON WAX TABLETS LIKE THESE.

and save your mother. Islam and the mercy of Allah await you."

"St. Martin!" Euric exclaimed angrily. "You never spoke like this before, when I went to your house to play with your sons."

"There was no need, then," said Fathma. "Now danger threatens. I have come as a friend to you, because you have eaten the bread of friendship with my sons."

"You will denounce me if I refuse?" he asked.

"Not if you will answer a question I must put to you," answered Fathma.

"What is the question?"

"Do you come here as a foe to the people of Islam?"

"Will you believe my answer?"

"The friend of my sons will not lie to their mother. A brave man will not lie to save his life."

Euric stared at her for a moment. The Arabs were stern like that. "I came to see my mother," he said, truthfully, "and to do no harm to the followers of the Prophet while I am here, Fathma Hanum."

"I believe you," she answered, "and I will say nothing of you until noon to-morrow. Will that give you time enough to go?"

"I shall leave," Euric answered, "when the gates are open at dawn."

"Wait till the second hour, it will be safer," said Fathma.

"The sun will be high."

"But there will be a crowd by then, women going down to wash in the river, and men to have grain ground at the mill and to fish and cut wood."

"You are right," said Euric. "I will wait until the second hour."

Mirela spoke suddenly, choosing her words as though it hurt her. "Euric came for more than that," she said. "You have taken his word that he came to do no harm to the enemies of the Prophet, and that is quite true, Fathma

Hanum. He did not come to do any harm, but to take me out
of the city, for the army of Pepin is marching here, and will
besiege Carcasona. There will be hunger and thirst, and
fighting in the streets if the city falls. I have chosen to stay,
but I give you now the chance to go."

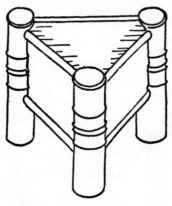

A STOOL THAT MIGHT HAVE BELONGED TO MIRELA.

Fathma sat down on a three-legged stool and leaned her
chin upon her hand while she thought. "When does this army
come?" she asked. "Or is that too much for you to tell,
Euric? Is it treason for you to tell me?"

"No," he answered, "though it was treason for my mother
to tell you so much as she did. Day after to-morrow they will
come. My father is the Count's man. If he learns that my
mother has told this to our enemies he will never return to
her."

"I do not believe that I have harmed the Count's cause overmuch," Mirela said, gravely, "and I have done for my friend what I would wish my friend to do for me. The Count and the Duke and Pepin himself should approve loyalty."

"Even a woman should know more of the business of war than that," Euric stormed.

"Cease, boy," Fathma said gently. "The lion makes a great roaring and wins praise for his valor, but the panther is silent and more deadly."

"Pooh!" said Euric, uneasily.

"I will send you a message, Euric," Fathma said, presently. "I do not yet know what it will be, but what I command, perform, and ask no questions. I promise that there will be no anger against you or your mother in the army of Pepin. That will be the thanks of the Arabs for the friendship of a Christian woman. Stay here, Euric, and wait for my message, even though you wait beyond the second hour to-morrow." She turned and went out, walking gracefully, her bearing and her clothes more elegant than he had remembered. He stood staring down at the fire, keeping instinctively to the lee side so that the smoke would not blow in his face.

"The meal has been ready a long time," said Mirela, quietly. "I was about to eat when you came. There is rabbit stew with herbs, and I found mushrooms for it yesterday, fresh, down by the river bank. I seldom have mushrooms since you went away, Euric. You used to gather them to dry, remember?"

"IN THE ARMY," SAID EURIC "WE EAT FROM THE POT,"

"Of course," he said, his voice troubled.

"What is the matter?" Mirela asked, putting the stew in two round wooden bowls with a wooden spoon in each. She handed one to Euric while she sat down on the long bench beside the dying fire.

"In the army," said Euric, "we eat from the pot."

"I keep to the Roman ways." Mirela smiled.

"We have little more than hard cakes and boiled pork and beer and cheese," said Euric. "This is better."

Mirela threw a few fagots on the embers for light, and blew on the flame with a long hollow reed. "It is late," she said. "The sun has gone down. We must go to bed."

"The men-at-arms," said Euric, "sometimes sit for half a candle after sunset, telling tales by the firelight. It is the best time of the day."

"The men-at-arms," said Mirela, dryly, "have wood in plenty for the cutting."

"Once," said Euric, "you had a bronze lamp with oil. There was a bit of wire to pull the wick. I burned my fingers to make it burn brighter."

"I still have the lamp," Mirela said, "but without husband or son I have been too poor to buy oil for it. I have used my oil and tallow for cooking and gone without lamp or rush-lights. Light is luxury."

"All that," Euric said proudly, "will be changed when the Count returns. Every one will be rich then."

"You have seen cities after a siege," said his mother. "You should know. Has that been true?"

"No," he answered, hesitatingly. "War is hard."

"Poverty follows in the path of destruction," Mirela said.

"You wish the Arabs to stay!" he cried suddenly, jumping up from his seat.

"For the good of our people I think I do," she answered slowly. "But my wish cannot help them to stay. They are not strong enough. There is food enough here for every one now,

MIRELA'S LAMP.

but not enough for a long siege. Part of the wall fell in the spring. The earth was washed from under it by the rain. Nor are there fighting men enough to stand against the armies of the Franks. The Arabs must go back across the Pyrenees to Hispania, but I think Fathma Hanum is right: there will be a thousand years of unhappiness for the land of the Gauls under Frankish rule. The year of our Lord seventeen hundred and fifty-one! How far away that sounds, does it not?"

"You are counting years, when it is minutes and hours that must be counted now. Fathma Hanum has gone to tell her husband that I am here and that Pepin the Short is coming."

"Yes," Mirela answered.

"You have betrayed me to them, and you talk about what will happen in a thousand years! The world will have come to an end by then. A thousand years is too great an age for even the earth to endure."

"No harm will come to you from the Arabs," Mirela said confidently. "Do you not remember that their pride is to be true friends and valiant enemies?"

"I am tired," Euric answered. "I would sleep."

Mirela went to a square chest that stood against the wall and drew out two thick, soft bearskins, which she laid on the floor. Then she laid a square woolen cloth over them. "You have not slept as soft and warm as this in two years, I'll wager," she said.

"I have had my cloak to wrap me in," he said. "But it will be good to lie on a bed again."

"It is good to have you back, my son." Mirela smiled at him.

But Euric was worried. "It would be better to be back if the Arabs knew nothing of my coming, and you and I were going to-morrow to the cave on the hillside where you would be safe until the siege is over."

He lay down, fully dressed, as was the army custom, except for his belt, with its heavy knife, and his oiled boots.

"Trust me and sleep," Mirela said. "Trust me, and may God and the Blessed Virgin watch over you and the holy

saints intercede for your sins!" She made the sign of the cross
over him, and he answered, sleepily, "Matthew, Mark, Luke,
and John, bless this house and those within!"

Euric did not wake until the early sunlight slanted through
the high windows into the room. Only once a day, during
bright days, was the room ever really light, for the windows
were not large, and the walls were of thick gray stone. Once
they had been painted over with white lime, but that had
flaked off and almost none remained. Euric sat up and
stretched. He had walked many miles the day before, and was
tired. The fire was already built. His mother had the iron
caldron with the rabbit stew that had been last night's supper
already heating for breakfast. He jumped up hungrily.

"Will you not wash before you eat?" Mirela asked re-
provingly.

"I forgot I was home again," he said. "In the army we do
not wash much."

"I know that," she said, "but let us leave army manners to
the army. There is water in the jar in the corner."

"That you carried from the well," he said.

"Yes."

"And all that to wash! The soldiers do not wash even
when they ford a stream."

Mirela laughed. "The Arabs would teach them," she said.
"In the days of the Romans there were great baths here. Our
cisterns were built then, and the pools in the courtyards of
the big houses. I am poor, but I am not too poor to have my
jar of cool water."

Euric washed his hands and face, and then they ate together, looking curiously at each other in the full light. Mirela was thinner, there were lines on her face, made by poverty and loneliness, and her hair was growing gray. Her dress, which had been made of good woolen stuff, was worn and patched, and the wide cloth girdle that served for pockets showed little of its once gay woven pattern. As he looked he realized suddenly that it was his absence and his father's

A WATER JAR LIKE MIRELA'S.

that had turned his mother's hair gray and lined her face with worry wrinkles. He leaned across and kissed her. She smiled at him, and they forgot the years between and talked again like mother and son. It seemed to Euric that he had never left that little house in Carcasona.

Mirela went out for water, and came back with a partridge she had bought from a boy in the street. "In honor of you," she said.

Before the second candle had burned to its end, a knock

sounded on the door and Mirela opened it. A black woman stood in the doorway and spoke to her, so low that Euric could not hear the words. Then Mirela closed the door, and came back. She stood silently reading the message written on a wax tablet in a hinged wooden frame. Euric waited impatiently.

"Holy St. Martin!" he cried after a moment or two. "What does it say?"

"That you are to wait until to-morrow and not leave this house until the second candle," Mirela said.

Euric stormed up and down the room. "How can I do that?" he cried angrily. "She says to wait, and does not say what I am to wait for. They will call me traitor when I go back. I came with a secret message for you, and you have betrayed my father's trust. What will come of it? This is war —I must leave and leave quickly. The Count must be warned that the Arabs are making ready. I must go!"

"Look first through the windows and see that there are not Arab guards in the street," said Mirela wisely.

Euric stood on the wooden chest and leaned out. He could see beyond the alley to the street. What he saw there made him jump back. There were no guards before the house, but at the entrance to the alley stood three Arab soldiers.

"Trapped!" he cried. "Trapped, Mother! Now you will see your son's head struck off by an Arab scimitar. Women know nothing of war and should learn to be silent when men give them orders. My father knew what is best, and if you had obeyed him all would have been well."

"All will yet be well," she replied tranquilly.

"You still believe that?" he asked.

"Yes. If it were not so they would have come to take you yesterday. Why should they wait? Do you think they are afraid of a woman and a boy?"

"I am a soldier of Pepin the Frank." Euric drew himself up proudly.

"Yes," Mirela answered, smiling, "but you will be a wiser soldier of Pepin the Frank next week, and stouter."

"I shall be dead next week," he mourned, "and no soldier at all."

"That may be," she replied, "if God wills. But Fathma Hanum will not have caused you harm."

"What can they do except make an ambush for the army?" Euric groaned. "I must get out and warn them."

"You cannot," his mother said. "Wait, Euric."

They waited quietly enough through the day. Euric tried to think of a way to kill three Arab soldiers without making a disturbance that would rouse the town. He could think of no way but prayer, so he kicked savagely at the fire platform. Its hard gray stone bruised his toe, and he sat down disconsolately. The world looked very black indeed. Mirela busied herself with the few simple tasks in the house, and then spun woolen thread with a distaff. She asked Euric to tell her the news of the court.

"They talk of making Pepin king," he said. "What matter he is only mayor of the palace by birth? His father was a great general, and the King is a do-nothing. There are many who wish him king, and all will wish it when he has driven out the Arabs. He has brought the nations together, he will conquer the whole world, and your Euric will be in his army. Are you not proud of that?"

PEPIN THE FRANK.

"Yes," said Mirela, smiling a little. "But a few minutes ago you thought you would be no soldier at all next week. Now you are setting out to conquer the whole world."

They slept that night as they had the night before, but not so long. Before daylight, at about the first candle, they were awakened by sounds in the street. Euric stood on the chest again to lean out of the window. Donkeys and mules and laden slaves marched past the end of the alley in a long, crowded line. They marched stumblingly until the dawn broke and gave them light to choose their steps. Even then there came some stragglers, and last a company of mounted soldiers. The three Arab guards at the end of the alley left their post, and the city grew as silent as though it were night. No bell had rung to tell that the first candle had burned to its end in the church where they kept the watch. Euric tried to find words, but his mother sang softly as she spun her thread.

"I will go out," said Euric.

"It is not yet the second-candle time," his mother warned.

"True," he agreed, "but I wish I knew what has happened."

At last the bell rang out. The second candle had been lighted. Euric ran to the door. Mirela dropped her distaff and followed him. The streets were full of Christians peering cautiously down alleys and looking over their shoulders as though they expected to see goblins behind them. They had all been told to stay indoors until the second candle, and had not dared to disobey. They searched, more and more boldly, but in the whole city there was not left a single Arab.

It was early afternoon when the army of Pepin burst from the woods on the other side of the river and rushed yelling toward the city. The Count had pushed to the front to get a first glimpse of his city. Euric was waiting for them beside the mill. His face was glowing with pride and with a new authority. He held up his hand to signal the party of nobles in shining armor of polished mail, riding their strong horses on high saddles of leather. The Count he had seen many times, but with him rode others he did not know. Among them was a simply-dressed man, small, but with commanding gray eyes and light hair that reached almost to his shoulders. Euric had begun to speak before he realized who the man with long hair must be, and then he gasped as he dropped to his knee. He was stopping, single-handed, the greatest army that the Western world had ever seen. He told his story to the Count, and the man with long hair smiled, his stern eyes suddenly growing gentle.

"Here is a fine thing!" he cried, and laughed. "I, Pepin, might have taken a year to drive out the infidels from Carcasona, and a woman has done it in a single night! Give the boy a horse and armor. He shall be a knight of France."

"That is great reward for me," Euric said boldly, "and I give you thanks. But it is small reward for my mother, who toils alone in a tiny house and spins for the bread she eats."

"What shall I give to her?" asked the great man. "Truly she shall have what she will."

"The house," said Euric, "where the Arab Moghazib and his wife, Fathma Hanum, have lived."

"Be it so," said Pepin, smiling. "You hear, Count Milon?"

"It shall be done," said the Count, and they rode on up the narrow path to the town.

And, except that the record of Mirela and Euric and Fathma Hanum is lost, that is exactly what happened when the army of Pepin marched against the Arabs in the year of our Lord 751, and Carcassonne became for the first time a city of France.

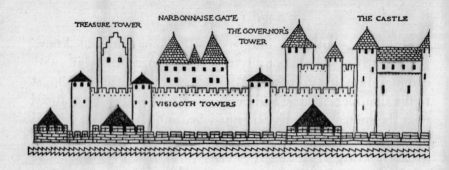

TREASURE TOWER   NARBONNAISE GATE   THE GOVERNOR'S TOWER   THE CASTLE

VISIGOTH TOWERS

Living Behind the Battlements

Did you know that some people live to-day in towns that have been buried for a thousand years? It sounds impossible, and yet it is quite true of a great many places in Europe, for the old buildings have been buried, and new ones built above them. Three of them, Carcassonne, Avignon, and Mont Saint-Michel, have been the homes of people who lived so long ago that no one knows exactly when they were founded. Parts of their oldest houses are buried under the newer ones where boys and girls listen to radios, or run outdoors into streets filled with automobiles as their mothers warn them to be careful.

But all the very old buildings in those towns are not buried underground. If they were it wouldn't be very exciting to go to see the cities above them. Fortunately for us, people have been living in those places continuously since the days of the most ancient peoples—Phœnicians, Carthaginians, Greeks, Romans, Gauls, Goths, and others too. People in Europe

28

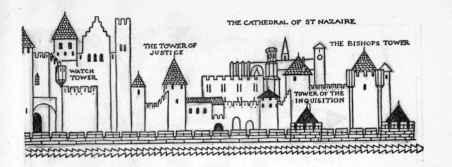

THE CATHEDRAL OF ST NAZAIRE

THE TOWER OF JUSTICE

WATCH TOWER

THE BISHOPS TOWER

TOWER OF THE INQUISITION

have no passion for tearing down buildings, as we seem to have. They go on living in them as long as the stones will stand on top of each other, and stones are hard and durable things.

Of these three cities Carcassonne is probably the oldest. It looks to-day as though knights in armor were about to descend from its battlements to walk about its narrow romantic streets with ladies in wimples of white gauze and girdles bright with jewels. You will wish you might take pictures of them with your kodaks, but the films will show only the places where they have passed.

In the story of Euric you saw the city become a part of the empire of the Franks when Pepin marched through its gates. Its single line of battlements was very ancient in his day, built by the Romans, strong and heavy in the massive Roman way. He approached it as you can, but more slowly, for he came on horseback, and you can drive in a swift car up to the great frowning gates, which are open to you as they were to him.

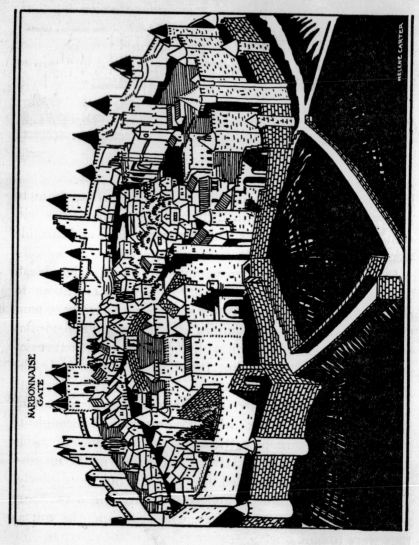

NARBONNAISE GATE

HELENE CARTER

THE CITY OF CARCASSONNE.

But you can see more than Pepin saw. Around that ancient line of Roman walls a later king of France, Louis IX, called St. Louis, built a second row of walls, pointed with towers like the first. There are fifty-four towers in the two circles of the walls and all of them, and the walls between, are full of ghosts. You need not be afraid of them, for the only chains they will rattle will be chain mail, and they will be far more likely to shout a welcome to you than to groan at you. They are the spirits of past ages, and from the great crowd of them we can choose one and follow him to learn how people lived in the ancient city. You have read a story about Euric and Mirela and Fathma and Pepin. There are a hundred other stories these ghosts can tell you, about the King—St. Louis—or the wicked old soldier Simon de Montfort, or the Black Prince. They all knew Carcassonne. Mostly they rode up to its walls on horseback, for they were nobles and loved horses, and of course there were no cars then. We will go by train or automobile. It will be less romantic, but quicker and more comfortable.

No matter how we go, by rail or highway, our smooth travel through the countryside will be suddenly livened by the sight, high on its hill, of the towers and battlements of the city of Carcassonne, with its crowd of ghosts waiting to welcome us back across the years into the ages when they lived.

They have been so often disturbed, those old ghosts! There have been so many changes in their old homes. For a time they were almost homeless, so terrible was the disrepair into

CARCASSONNE · TO~DAY

which their city fell. Now it is all fresh and gay again, and of course the ghosts are much happier.

They will tell us to leave our twentieth-century luggage at a modern hotel, either behind the battlements, or in the new city (it is six hundred years old, but don't tell the ghosts you think that is old—they might be offended). If we are hungry, the hotels of Carcassonne can offer wonderful food. One of the nicest kinds is a high round cake that looks like an American layer cake with white icing. After dinner it will be passed around with a knife with which you can cut a piece as large as you like. But it isn't a layer cake, it is solid nougat candy, sweet and full of nuts and citron. If you are in a hurry to talk to the ghosts behind the battlements, you might take your nougat with you and eat it on the way. There will be no use in offering to share it with the ghosts; there was no such thing in their day, and they do not like new things. In fact, it is best not to talk to them about any of the things they did not have. There are quite a lot of them: gasoline, and automobiles, and electricity, and steam power—even windmills should not be mentioned to the older ghosts. Then cotton goods and silk were rare curiosities, there was no tobacco, no coffee or chocolate, no peaches, or paper, of course no printing, or tomatoes, or turkeys, or cranberry sauce, and, above all, no airplanes, and no forks.

And so, remembering not to offend our friendly ghosts by talking about things they cannot understand, we will go through the great ancient gate of the Porte Narbonnaise— which is opposite the one by which Euric entered the city

THE NARBONNAISE GATE.

—and choose a ghost to explain it all to us. Euric and Mirela
and Fathma are not here to-day, so we will choose a knight
who came into Carcassonne in the retinue of Pepin. He has
a jolly, friendly face, but the first thing he says as he hails us
is that he does not like the outer walls. He says they are too
modern and spoil the city. They were built six hundred years
ago, at the same time as the "new" city on the plain below,
but that is very new to this twelve-hundred-year-old ghost.
The new walls are quite as romantically beautiful as the older
inner line, and they are much neater, for there are not three
kinds of masonry to be seen in them, but only one—besides
the recent repairs.

The ghostly knight will toss his head, on which is a chain-
mail cap that clinks pleasantly, and if any one agrees with
him that the outer walls have spoiled the city, he will immediately disagree a little proudly, and say that they may be
new, but at least they made the city almost impossible to capture. He will point out the strength of the entrance, with its
two flanking towers and its great drawbridge over a moat,
and then prove his point by leading the way along the inner
walls to the Porte d'Aude, by which Euric entered the city.
When we want to stop to look at the castle that guards its
entrance, he will urge us to wait until we have seen the place
where the barbican used to be.

"Barbican?" we ask. "What is a barbican?"

"None of the people of your day know that," he replies,
pleased. "Your people and my people have a lot in common,
and that is one reason why I like your people so much better

THE·BARBICAN·AND·OUTER·WALLS·BUILT·BY·KING·LOUIS·THE·NINTH

than the people who lived between my time and yours. We never had barbicans in my day, either. Still, it was a good invention. Especially here, where the river is so near. There should have been fortifications commanding it in my day. That is what the barbican was for. It is a round wall connected with a fortress. In this case it was a separate round fort connected with the city by a fortified passage. You can see the passage now, but the barbican was torn down one time while I was away. I have been told that the stones in it were used to build houses with." He shakes his mailed head until the links rattle again, disapprovingly. Below the battlements a still-fortified stairway leads down toward the river, to the place where the barbican once was. It is almost a fortress itself.

"Life must be very dull nowadays," the ghost says, sympathetically. "They tell me that when people want more money nowadays they have to work for it. That is terrible. In my day we just raised an army and went out after it. I wasn't powerful enough to try it alone, but I've often gone in the armies of others. And we would capture some castle or city, and get plenty of money."

"Some one had to do the work," you suggest.

"Oh, yes," he agrees indifferently, "workmen, tradespeople, and farmers. But we had all the fun, doing the fighting. And when there wasn't a war we could pretend there was, and play at jousting with a friend, or get a great noble to hold a tourney and offer a fine prize to the best knight. I won this armor at a tourney"—he shows it proudly—"and

THE WATCH TOWER.

a beautiful horse. Unfortunately the horse is gone now, but really he knew almost as much about fighting as I did."

Again he leads the way down a narrow flight of stone stairs from the top of the inner walls, and shows the network of passages, almost a labyrinth, leading from the gate in the outer wall to the courtyard of the castle. It is so narrow and there are so many gateways in it that you understand sud-

AN AX AND A HAMMER USED IN EURIC'S TIME.

denly why castles of the Middle Ages were so very hard to capture. There were twenty places where a single man could stop a hundred. He could shield himself behind a thick oaken door, and with a bow and arrow or a sword do a lot of damage, one by one, to the attackers, who would have no room to mass against him. But if we admire the castle too extravagantly the old ghost will say that in his day the building was not at all like this.

"We were too proud to hide behind barricades all the time," he explains. "We built ourselves a donjon—"

"To put your prisoners in?" we ask.

"No, indeed," he says. "In my day a donjon was the chief home of a noble. He might own country houses besides, but he had to have a donjon to go to when he was attacked by his neighbors. In later times, the sort of people who built these outer walls and this castle used our old donjons for prisons, because they were so strong. In our day," and he draws himself up proudly, "we did not require so much space or comfort." And he gives the scornful glance of a man who could ride forty miles a day through mud and dust halfway to his horse's knees, and be ready at the end of his journey for an evening of backslapping and singing, or a game of chess by the dim light of candles or smoky lamps.

He leads through the castle, pointing out the entrance to the great hall where the military lord of Carcassonne sat in judgment, or received his friends in the evenings, and the stables, and the place where the weavers and spinners did their work, and the carpenter shop, and the ironmonger's, and the sheepfold. "At least, that is where it used to be. There were no sheep in it except in time of siege. At other times they stayed down in the fields, of course. But the rest of the castle was a lively place enough."

He leads through the inner gate of the castle, into the city itself. "That was another barbican," the knight says, pointing to a round projection from the protective wall of the castle. "They built them frequently. Not a bad idea, I must admit, though I like our simple ways better. And here is the city." He points with pride around him. "It wasn't much like this in my day, though there is one bit of street I often go to, and imagine that I am back again, and nothing has changed. Come, I will show it to you."

He stalks off, and only a few blocks from the castle stands against one wall of a very narrow crooked little street. Standing just there, we seem, indeed, to be in a city that is very

A BATTERING-RAM.

ancient. The sun cannot quite shine into the slitlike opening except at midday, and from somewhere comes an odor of garlic and strong cheese and hot soup.

"Come," the ghost says sadly, "it makes me too homesick to stay here. It even smells the way it used to."

"Was all the city just narrow streets like that?" we ask.

"Oh, no," he says, "of course not. There were several wide squares, and an open space in front of nearly all the churches. We had lots of churches in my day. But we had none of these things you call shops." He points scornfully to places where postcards and souvenirs are displayed for sale, ticketed with their prices. "In our day a shop was as it should be, a place where honest workmen made honest goods and bargained for them with honest buyers. Armor, and woven stuffs, and jewelry, and baked bread, and wine and cheese. But most of the buying was done once a week at the market. It was held in the square, and there the farmers grouped themselves in one space, and the weavers in another, and so on, so that you

COINS MADE BY PEPIN.

could compare their offerings, and select the one that pleased you most. Market day was very gay and every one enjoyed it. At least, they did when the Count's taxes were not so high that there was little left to sell in Carcasona."

"Carcasona," we repeat.

"We called it so in my day," he answers.

"What does that mean, Carcasona?"

He smiles, delighted at the chance to show his knowledge. "In the ancient days," he says, "there was a city in Africa called Carthage. It was very rich and powerful and sent ships to trade with the people of this land. There was only forest and wilderness here then and the people lived in caves, but the traders from Carthage built a trading-post here, with a wall around it. It is said that in their language 'cars' meant city, and 'casso' meant walled. It may have been smaller than the city the Gauls built here afterward, and it is certain it was somewhat smaller than the Roman city. That was the third one. The Romans were great builders, and polite, clever people. But after a time they were conquered by the Goths, who were tall blond men, like me." The ghost smiles and draws himself up to a great height. He has yellow hair and blue eyes, and a splendid figure. "The heathen Arabs came next.

"We didn't let them stay here long," he says. "The Gothic Count Milon begged Pepin to help him drive them out, and Pepin gathered a great army. I was proud to be with them. Among us were Burgundians, Franks, and men from many other nations. I am afraid you would not know who they all were if I should tell you their names." He shakes his head again, sadly. "Anyway, Count Milon did not lose his independence, though he had to acknowledge allegiance to Pepin for his help. But he retained the ancient right of the Counts of Carcassonne to coin money here in their own name. That was something to be proud of."

We ask the ghost, suddenly, where he went to school, and he laughs heartily. "Why," he says, "no one went to school in my day except monks and such. When I was eight years old I was sent as a page to the court of the Count Milon, and there I learned all the manly arts, as any young man of

RACE MAP
of EUROPE

ANGLO~
SAXONS

FRIESIANS
SAXONS

GOTHS

NORMANS

FRANKS

MONT
SAINT MICHEL

BURGUNDIANS

GAULS

RIVE

AQUITANIANS. AVIGNON

CARCASSONNE

R

BLACK·SEA

VISIGOTHS

ARABS

ROMANS

D
A
N
U
B
E

ROME

M
E
D
I
T

ARABS

A
F
R
I
C
A

R
A
N
E
A
N   SEA

ARABS

knightly birth should do. I learned to carve the meat at my lord's table, to train and care for horses, to ride and joust. While I was young, of course I was forced to use wooden arms until I was given a sword and shield for my own by the Count. Perhaps even you have heard of the custom of the vigil? When we were old enough and skillful enough to bear arms, we prayed a whole night through at the altar, and in the morning our liege lord—mine was Count Milon, and a better never lived—gave us a shield and a sword and the embrace of the accolade, as a welcome into the company of knights. That was the good old custom. In the days when these outer walls were built it had changed somewhat, and the lords had become too penurious to give every knight a sword and shield. They made the young men supply their own as best they could."

He goes on to explain how very grim and warlike and direct and manly the people of his day were, not interested in pretty homes, or in double walls to their cities, or the too-heavy armor that later came into fashion—and you will be reminded a little of Buffalo Bill and the Western settlers of our own country. Probably they were not so very different, builders of a new nation, fighting fierce and hostile enemies hand to hand, admiring personal bravery and strength and loyalty more than any other virtues.

But we mustn't let our thoughts wander away from what our knightly Buffalo Bill is telling us. We have reached the inner walls now, near the Tower of the Bishops. "It wasn't always inhabited by bishops," he explains. "In wartime the bishop had to go somewhere else, and the windows he had cut in the outer walls were filled up again with stone. Here is a fine old staircase built inside the tower wall. Good enough for any one, even a bishop, but you should have heard the fussing that went on because a certain priest once thought there should be a broad staircase in the 'modern' manner.

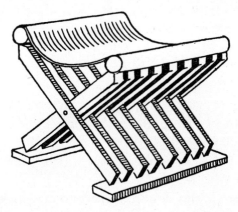

A FOLDING STOOL IN ONE OF THE TOWERS.

Our men-at-arms used to build their fires in the middle of the room, where it would warm all parts equally, and make plenty of room to sit around it in a circle in the good old way. While we were on duty the men did their cooking at the center fires, heated water, and melted lead to pour down on the enemy."

"Where did the smoke go?" we ask.

The old ghost laughs. "That," he says, "is the silly problem that the people who built all the hooded fireplaces against side walls used to worry about. Why, the smoke went up, of course, where it naturally would go. It made all our ceilings a fine deep black, solid and even. Of course some of it escaped, and some of it we breathed. It made us strong, too. We

FIREPLACE OF PEPIN'S TIME.

always took great pride in being strong, and never fretted about such details as smoke."

You will wonder how breathing a lot of smoke could make men strong, and that will lead you to wonder how many people breathed the smoke, and how many men it took to hold a city like Carcassonne during a siege.

"About three thousand," the ghost answers. "A few less in my day, when there was only one circle of walls, and a few more later, because the outer circle is somewhat larger than our old line of defense. They did not man the inner walls, of course, after they built the outer ones. They used the space between for exercise and tourneys. Very inefficient. We had an open space in front of the donjon. It was much more convenient."

"What did they call that space?" we ask. "Was that the lists?"

"Of course," the ghost says. "It is *lices* in French. It sounds like the word for lilies, so perhaps it meant a field of lilies. It certainly was a field, but it is another of those words like the name of our old Tresau Tower over there. That one, see? Yes, that's it. The word sounds like 'treasure,' so there are people who will tell you that it was once used to guard treasure, or that there is treasure buried under it. A lot of people have even wasted a lot of good time digging around it trying to find treasure. All they found were a few old coins that had been dropped by passers-by. Of course it may have been a treasure tower once, for all I know. I haven't stayed here all through the ages. But never when I have been here has there been any treasure there that any one told me anything about."

"Then what does the word mean?" we ask.

"I'm sure I haven't the least idea," he replies scornfully. "Ask some monk. They concern themselves with unimportant things like words. I have too many wars on my mind to bother with words."

"I suppose there were a great many wars in Carcassonne," we say, hoping he will tell us about them.

"Oh, yes, indeed," he agrees happily. "If you could only see some of the fights that have taken place in these very streets, and on these walls! Often and often I go to the spot where some good fight took place, and imagine it just as it was. Other people who don't know, but only imagine them, do the same. A little while ago some of them built an open-air theater over there near the Church of St. Nazaire, beside the Tower of the East Mill. They give shows there about our Carcasona history. They are very pretty, but they never fool me at all. I can see quite well that they never really kill anybody, but only pretend to, and the girls aren't nearly so pretty as some I can remember in my day. It is like the *hourdes* over there on the wall. See them?"

"What are *hourdes*?" we ask.

"Those wooden shelters built on the top of the walls," the ghost explains, and he leads the way toward them so rapidly that we almost have to run to keep up with him. He comes to a place where, on the top of the stone parapet, a long wooden passage has been built on the wall. He points up to it and shows how it was made.

"Of course," he explains, "this wasn't built for a real siege, because there is nothing but peace hereabouts now. It is too bad, because they have really built the *hourdes* very well. Quite as well as we did. On this part of the wall, where they did not put them up, you can see the holes that we made in the walls, ready for the braces—those square holes. You see how firmly the braces held the wooden platforms in place, and how well the whole affair could shield the soldiers? Just

HOURDES ARE WOODEN SHELTERS BUILT ON THE TOP OF THE WALLS.

small slits to shoot through, a roof over your head, and square holes in the floor to drop stones through, and pour down melted lead on the enemy! How they would run! That was great sport.

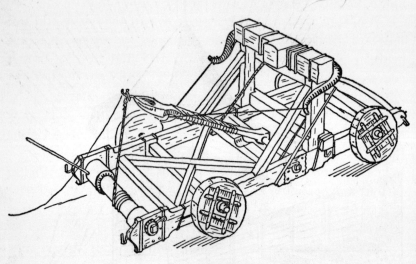

A BALLISTA.

"And we never lacked ammunition, because after our own arrows were all shot, we only had to pick up those the besiegers had sent to us and shoot them back again. The same with stones. While we threw all our loose ones at them, they were throwing quite as many at us, so we gathered them up and threw them back again. Their object was to batter holes in our walls, and ours to keep them far enough away so they could not. They brought ballistas and battering-rams and catapults to hammer at the walls. That is how the Arabs got in. They knocked so many holes in the walls that our people had scarcely anything left to defend. But they never did much to repair the ruins, so when our good Pepin led us against the city they ran away in the night.

"We were always just a little ashamed that we could not tell our grandchildren about the time we vanquished the heathen. A few people tried to pretend that we did, but of course there wasn't much sense to that." He sighs at that lost opportunity. "Besides, they had fine weapons, hardened by what we thought was an enchantment, though now I know they were just steel. Ours were only of iron, and not very sharp."

We remember some stories of enchanted weapons—King Arthur's Excalibur was the most famous, but there were plenty of others—and we are glad to know the reason for the "enchantment."

As we walk on around the walls, our friendly ghost tells the names of the different towers, the Tower of the Inquisition, the Tower of the Governor. One is the Tower of the Carpenters, and there are two Mill Towers. You will know by their names that they were more than mere places from which stones and arrows could be hurled at an enemy. They were workshops and houses and barracks. And they are there still, as they were in the ghost's day, and have been for all the days since.

"Didn't you have any amusements?" we ask, because it has all sounded pretty warlike so far.

"Of course we did," he answers. "We even had a play every year, something like the ones your people give in the open-air theater. A priest used to read the Gospel story of Christmas to us, and young men carefully chosen acted in pantomime the parts of Joseph and Mary and the Wise Men and the Shepherds, and sang like the angels. It was very beautiful. Then we had wandering story-tellers and dancers and acrobats that used to come to market places and castles

SHOES THAT BELONGED TO CHARLEMAGNE, PEPIN'S SON.

to gather in a few coins. There was one story they used to tell that I liked very much. It was about a very beautiful girl named Cinderella, who—"

"Oh, we know that one!" we interrupt. "Her fairy god-mother gave her glass slippers and—"

But then the ghost interrupts us. *"Glass?"* he repeats. "Now isn't that absurd? How could she dance in glass slippers? Her slippers were of squirrel skin, of course, the very nicest and softest material for a lady's slippers. *Vair*, we

called it. Oh, now that may be what you mean by 'glass.'
Vair, squirrel fur—*verre*, glass. Yes, that is the trouble. You
should always talk in French, then you wouldn't make such
a mistake."

CINDERELLA'S COACH.

But we disagree with him there, for whenever we talk in
French some one says we do make mistakes!

"She had a coach," the ghost continues. "We didn't think
much of coaches in those days. We didn't waste our time
fussing about roads the way you do. A little mud and dust
makes you strong, and delays enemies who may want to
attack you. Coaches need smooth roads. We did a lot of

traveling, but knightly folk usually rode horseback. It was more comfortable. Our coaches had no brakes to hold them back downhill, so the driver had to get out and help or tie the wheels. Oh, we managed well enough, and without reading about it in books, either, the way you do. Our books were worth something. They were in Latin, so very few people could read them. As they were written by hand, the pages made of fine parchment, very expensive, and the bindings of precious materials, they were something to own without troubling about what was written in them."

By that time we are getting hungry, and the ghost is surprised. "If you would get up at dawn, as I do," he says, "and go to bed at sundown, or a little later, you would eat at better hours. We used to have our breakfast as soon as we woke up, our dinner at ten in the morning, and our supper at four in the afternoon. Now it is only noon and you are hungry, just when I was going to show you the most interesting things here."

"Tell us how you ate your meals, instead," we suggest, and again the old ghost laughs.

"First a servant brought in two trestles," he explains, "and then another brought in the board, and put it on the trestles. That is what we called setting the table."

"With nothing on it?" we ask, surprised but realizing suddenly why we say "board," meaning meals.

"Of course," says the ghost. "The table being set, some one would put the saltcellar on it, and hang a cloth across the front, because we did not think it delicate to see dogs gnawing the bones we threw them."

"You left the top of the table bare?" we ask.

"Why not?" The ghost is quite disgusted. "You wouldn't want to put a piece of hot meat on a cloth, would you?"

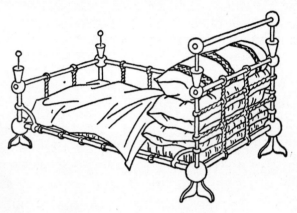

PEPIN SLEPT IN A BED LIKE THIS.

"You might put it on a plate," we suggest.

But the ghost does not like plates. He never used them, and feels that fingers and the bare table are quite good enough. He carries a knife at his belt to cut what needs cutting, and he can pull out of the pot whatever he fancies. He even has a wooden spoon, prettily carved by hand of pear wood, and feels it a very elegant implement indeed. He tells us that he always ate either in the kitchen or—in the houses of the greatest nobles, who had a separate kitchen—in the hall. When he was being especially honored he ate in the bedroom, because it was, he explains, the most formal room in the house. The hall was the public room, but the bedroom belonged exclusively to the owner's family. Only favored guests were asked into it, whereas any passer-by expected to be admitted to the hall.

The ghost has told us almost all he can. He was a fighting man, and knew nothing about the things we spend so much time learning in school—reading and writing and arithmetic. We must find some other ghost to tell us about those things. We might stop at the Governor's Tower and see if we cannot find some monkish man of business there to tell us about the arithmetic of his day. It was very different from ours, for the old Christians did not use the numerals we do, which came to us from the Arabs. The old way was by means of Roman numerals. We were taught in school how to read them, but not to add them. There was an I for 1, a V for 5, an X for 10, an L for 50, a C for 100, and so on. It would not be any use to write them down under each other to add them together, for you would have to do it all in your head, anyway. There must be some other means of counting. People in Pepin's day had a row of little cups into which

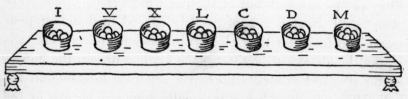

ONE WAY OF COUNTING.

they threw pebbles, or an abacus. They worked on exactly
the same principle. The cups were arranged as you see them
in the picture, so that the first represented units, the second
fives, the third tens, and so on. If you had thirty-two to add
to forty-four, you didn't just add two to four, and four to
three, because no one had thought of that easy way. Instead,
you threw two pebbles and then four pebbles into the units

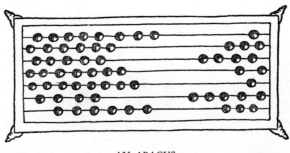

AN ABACUS.

cup, and three and then four into the tens cup. Then you
took out five of the tens pebbles and put one in the fifties
cup, and five from the units cup, and put one in the fives cup.
Then you wrote down one letter for each pebble. It would
come to LXXVI. You try it with a row of teacups and some
beans. It is slow and clumsy, but it works.

So did the abacus, which works a little quicker as you
throw the beads across the wires they are strung on—instead
of putting pebbles into cups—but if you shake it you lose
the count. An abacus is rather fun to play with. Let us try

counting the years from the time of Pepin on one, and imagine we are floating across the lovely land of France, just as our ghost can do. When we come to a place or a time we like, we can shake the abacus and stop, and having stopped and lost our count of years, we can stay for a little in some other time and place—and so we go down the years . . . click, click, click . . . one, two, three . . .

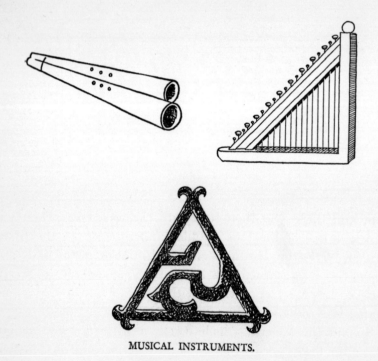

MUSICAL INSTRUMENTS.

Avignon

The Battlements of the Popes

"Realm and Empire!"

"OPEN in the name of the King of France!" said a man's voice outside the door. The children stopped eating at the sound, and Jehanne patted her new red ribbon proudly. "Visitors!" she thought, "and I of all the family am dressed in my best to receive them!"

Régnier, her father, rose smiling from the table where he sat at breakfast with his family and his apprentice. The tone of the voice had been gruff, but the name of the King of France made it a welcome one. Some officer of the King would give an order for another gate, no doubt, even before the first was finished. A hurried order, perhaps, for which he could charge an extra price.

Benezet, the apprentice, had jumped to throw up the bar of the door, and Régnier and his wife and the children, all but the baby, were standing expectantly behind him, all interest and pleasant politeness. Noble visitors were welcome. They brought prosperity to the poor. Benezet had the bar up, and flung open the door.

Into the room marched a large man, roughly dressed, with a short sword by his side, and a leathern jacket with small metal studs sewn on it. He did not look like a buyer of wrought-iron gates.

"In the name of the King, Régnier Paesse," he said harshly, "you are ordered to present yourself at the south gate of the Fort St. André to-morrow at sunrise, there to join the forces of the King, which march to the defense of his realm against the army of the English."

There was a lot more, but Jehanne could not comprehend it very well. Every one spoke so quickly, her mother half screaming, the baby wailing loud because the others were disturbed. Jehanne felt that her heart would stop beating if she did not cry, but she could not. Her father was to go away from them! She forgot even her new red ribbon in this calamity. The big soldier was speaking quickly, sharply, trying to drown out the other voices. When he had done he turned and walked out of the house. He held in his hand a long roll of paper, on which the names of other unlucky bourgeois of the King were written. He had spoken with a strange northern accent, very different from the soft Provençal that Jehanne and her family spoke.

Benezet closed the door again, and threw the bar across it, saying nothing. Jehanne's eyes burned with holding back her tears. Her mother and the baby and her father were all talking or screaming so loudly that it scarcely seemed worth while to add a word to the din. Benezet was a good boy, though sometimes he played pranks and teased her. He was

A CANDLESTICK OF ENAMEL.

like an older brother, so Jehanne took his hand and held it.
Her father said he was a good apprentice. He was learning
fast how to heat the iron and beat it into lovely rounded
forms and twisted patterns, and to make joints neatly, for
great gates and candlesticks, or cooking-ladles, or pike heads
and arrowheads. He could blow the great bellows and keep
the fire bright and hot, and chop wood, and still find breath
to whistle gayly at his work. His hand was strong, and it
squeezed hers until she jerked away lest he break the bones.

Jehanne's mother was crying, "And what will happen to
you in the army, my husband? And what will happen to us
with you gone? You will be killed by the terrible English, or
made to shoot one of those devilish *batons à feu* that blow
into bits as often as not, they say. Oh, the Virgin keep you
from meddling with such contrivances! There's nothing noble
in war these days. Gunpowder, and the firing it in cannon!

What horrible thing will men invent next for killing one another? War was once fought hand to hand, and beautiful to see, with armor shining bright and plumes waving. But will the knights wear plumes to be burned by smoking powder? And will the soldiers march with gay songs to a battle that will be horrible with the noise of hideous cannon? Oh, Régnier, do not go, do not go! We shall starve and you will be killed."

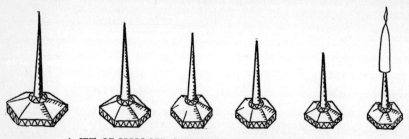

A SET OF HOLLOW CANDLESTICKS FOR TRAVELING.

"What can I do but go?" Régnier asked, miserably enough. "The King has called me, and I must. I am his vassal, for I have bought lease of his land. I must go when he calls me to arms. The saints know I do not wish to go. If I could I would stay at home, but what can I do? These northern officers are strangers here, they care nothing for my protests, only to send the King full companies of strong men. And the King is far away, in Paris, most likely. What does he care for a simple ironwright of Villeneuve, at the edge of his realm?"

"And we might have lived as easily in Avignon, safe in

the Empire," his wife sobbed on, "where the good Queen Jehanne of Naples is liege lady, and the Emperor overlord. Their vassals are left in peace since the popes have dwelt there. Just across the river in the Empire men live in safety, while here you are torn from your family to fight against the English, who have done nothing to you. And my brother is safe with his family in Avignon. Safe, and why?"

Régnier answered regretfully: "When we took this place it seemed so fitted to our purpose. The garden, the shop, with space enough to execute a large commission if one should be given me, the house, the well of good water—all so cheap. And across the river, in the city of the popes, all so crowded, so expensive, and the noble visitors' men-at-arms fighting in the street when they could think of nothing else to do, or the Pope's guards looked the other way. How should we see that here war would strike, while all remained peaceful across the river?"

Jehanne's mother was sobbing more softly. "We have been so happy here!" she cried over and over again, hanging on her husband's blue tunic as though she would tear it in her grief. "The boatmen shout, 'Realm!' and, 'Empire!' to steer their boats to right or left, but never did I think we should use those terms to steer our lives to peace or war, to happiness or misery! Just a little river flows between. And we have been so happy here!"

"Perhaps," suggested Benezet, "when they discover you are an ironwright they may put you to work mending armor and putting wheels to wagons and new heads to lances, instead of fighting. There must be scarcity of good ironwrights in the King's army as much as elsewhere."

"What help is that?" demanded Régnier, miserably. "It may, to be sure, save my life, but if my family have meanwhile starved to death I would liefer die than come home at last to an empty hearth."

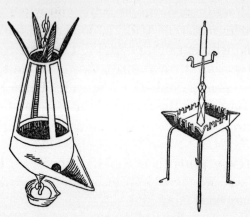

A LAMP AND A CANDLESTICK OF IRONWORK.

"Could I not go in your stead?" asked Benezet hopefully. "I should like to see the English, and fight with the army. There was an English lord last year at Avignon. I saw him. His face was red and smiling, and his men were stout lads and spoke a strange French."

"You are too young, Benezet. They would not take you."

"I am fifteen," said Benezet, "and many have gone to war younger. I could say I was seventeen, and that would be old enough."

" 'Tis I was called," Régnier answered. "And in any case, you could not go. I took you as apprentice to learn my trade. As your master I am responsible for your safety. Now you will return to your father, and I will give back your apprentice fee."

Jehanne's mother wailed again. "That will beggar us!" she cried. "I had forgotten that. The last iron you bought, and all that half-finished gate, so long in the working—oh, Régnier, who will finish that? And until it is done no one will pay for it."

"At least," Benezet urged, "I can stay here and finish the gate. I am sure I can teach myself to do it. I have watched you so often, Master. I need only a little practice, then I could do it."

"Only a few years' practice," Régnier smiled, sadly. "No, Benezet. You and your apprentice fees go back to your father. He worked hard and saved that you might learn a trade, and I accepted the money to teach you. Since I cannot, back you go, with the money to make a new start."

His wife nodded, through her sobs. "Oh, yes, that must be," she said. "If we must starve we will do it honestly. Oh, if only these kings could share the misery they cause with their silly wars! What have we to do with them? And what care we for England, or even for King John?"

"Be quiet!" cautioned Régnier. "Such words are treason. King John of France is our liege lord, and we must honor and obey him."

"We never saw him," said his wife, stubbornly, "nor he

us. He sends to us once a year for taxes, and does not even have the grace to send honest men, but makes us pay as much to their greed as for the King's dues. If this war were to fight against the King, I'd let you go willingly."

"Treason, treason—be quiet!" Régnier begged. "Do you want us all hanged from the battlements?"

"As well hang as starve," she answered. "It's quicker done."

Jehanne shuddered at the thought of hanging, and walked to the door. The sun was shining just above the top of the Pope's towers across the river. It made the great pile of masonry look grim and black and bigger than ever. The bridge of St. Benezet across the swift river was bathed in the cool early rays. It had been broken for a year, and was but newly mended by the Pope. Two boats were coming downstream, moving very rapidly in the current. Jehanne could see their boatmen guiding them with oars so that they should not be crushed against the piers of the bridge. They shouted as they came, "Realm!" when they wished to steer for the right bank, and "Empire!" for the left. Realm and empire! The bridge connected them, but did not unite them. The Pope connected them, too, like a bridge of religion, but he also could not unite them.

The boatmen passed under the bridge, probably cursing it as a menace to their passage down the strong current. The people of Villeneuve and Avignon gave continuous thanks to St. Benezet, who built the bridge three hundred years ago, and to the Pope for keeping it in repair. In gratitude half

the boys of Avignon were named for the good saint of
the bridge. In the old days the city people were drowned
crossing in little boats that upset. Now the rivermen upset
against the bridge piers. What was good for one was bad for
another. Jehanne stood in the sunlight thinking that out.
Perhaps this English war would be good for some one—the
King, perhaps. To her it seemed quite senseless. The King
of England wished to make himself King of France as well,
though he was already Duke of Aquitaine, and that should
be enough for one man. He, with his beautiful jewels and
clothes made of silks and soft cotton stuffs and furs, he could
ride proud, prancing horses, and be waited on by servants.
He was the lord of great estates, and when he passed poor,
humble folk must bow or kneel to him as to all great folk.
It would be strange to be noble.

Jehanne took a few steps forward, imagining how she
would walk swishing a long-tailed dress behind her, wearing
a jeweled headdress with wimple and veil, and heavy rings
on her hands—kept white, the sun never allowed to touch
them. The gown would be heavy and uncomfortable, and
the sun was too pleasant to shut out. If only the rich would
leave poor folk alone no one would mind them very much.
Why did the saints allow them power to ruin the happiness
of honest poor folk? Millions owed allegiance to the King,
and only the Pope and the people of Heaven could call him
to account for his deeds.

The sun rose a little higher and bathed the river in gold.
Her uncle would be painting now in the palace, helping the

TOWER·OF·PHILIP·THE·FAIR

great Matteo Giovannetti make the pictures on the walls of
the Pope's great Audience Hall. Or had they finished with
that, and already started to work on the great chapel above?
It was a long time since she had seen her uncle. Such a gentle
man, and so finely dressed. Not like noble folk, of course, but
his clothes were of such bright colors. His wife's father was
a dyer.

The sobbing and the sounds of terrified misery came to
Jehanne from the house. Only the Pope could save them—
no one else. She sighed, and then began walking slowly down
the hill toward the Tower of King Philip. She was afraid of
it, it looked so menacing, forever guarding the entrance to
the bridge. But this time she would not heed her fear. What

was a tower built of stones? The men-at-arms were men like
her father. Or perhaps they were more like that rough officer
who had told her father he must fight against the English.
She held her head up and walked doggedly toward the tower.
Then she ran, because the day was fine, and it was a silly
waste of a good chance not to run down the hill. So she came
quickly to the tower, and the men-at-arms glanced up from
their dice game, but said nothing to her as she passed by
them through the wide double gates, and came out on the
arched roadway of the bridge.

This was where folk danced gayly up and down over the
arches, making a sport of the jolly, noisy farandole. She
could see them from her house, and hear the music when the
wind was right. They danced sometimes at night by the light
of torches, breathlessly—or in the afternoon. The visiting
nobles had so many companies of musicians in their train,
who gladly played for the common people and passed their
caps afterward for coins, Jehanne decided she would dance
upon the bridge when she had grown a little bigger. Her
mother said no, but later perhaps she would let her.

As she came up the slope of the last arch but one, Jehanne
slowed her steps. Ahead was the guardian gateway and tower
of the walls of Avignon. Who was she to approach the palace
of the superior of kings? What could the fate of one humble
family be to a personage who bore the fate of the whole
Christian world on his shoulders? What could a child mean
to the patron of the greatest men of learning, a child who

sometimes forgot to say her prayers, or grumbled at the dullness of the mass? She stopped. Just ahead was the tiny chapel of St. Nicholas, and she took a little heart from that, because St. Nicholas was a generous saint. When he lived on earth he distributed all his wealth among the poor, and now that he had joined the company of Heaven he still brought gifts to poor children on his own day. He was a protector of travelers, a friend to children. Perhaps he would listen if she prayed to him. She was a traveler, she was traveling from one city to another, from one fief to another, from a realm to an empire, even though it was just across a single bridge.

She went into the small chapel. It was cool and peaceful there after the warm sun on the open bridge, with the rushing river below. She dropped down before a painted figure of the saint, who stared at her impersonally—his eyes were painted, too. She murmured a prayer in Latin, then told her troubles in French, but he never moved. Carved wood he was, and gave no sign that he had heard or cared.

"I ask no miracle," she begged, "just that my uncle may have influence with Master Giovannetti, and Master Giovannetti with the Pope, and that between them they may ask the King to let my father stay with us. So many plans we have made, good St. Nicholas. Perhaps you did not know about the gate? It is only half finished, and will be a great credit when it is done. I beg you, good St. Nicholas, never bring me sweetmeats again, or notice me all my life—only this one

FORT SAINT ANDRÉ
VILLENEUVE

TOWER OF
PHILIP THE FAIR

RHONE

BRIDGE OF
SAINT BENEZET

CHAPEL OF
St NICHOLAS

RIVER

THE
PALACE OF THE
POPES

A VIEW OF JEHANNE'S PATH FROM VILLENEUVE TO THE POPE'S PALACE

time! Oh, if prayers bring you joy in Heaven, mine shall be said in all earnestness, and often. Oh, I know that once you were a great noble and a bishop, but you never lost your care for the poor. Holy St. Nicholas, I have no offering for you, but you have ever given freely. Give me my father, only, dear St. Nicholas. Please, please!"

Tears were falling on her hand, and she feared her bright-red ribbon would be spotted. She wiped away the tears and looked down to see, and then she smiled, for she had an offering, after all. Quickly she undid the ribbon and held it toward the figure of the saint. "Oh, good St. Nicholas," she begged, "perhaps you do not care for ribbons, but it is all I have. I have not even a coin to buy a candle for you. Do not despise me, good St. Nicholas! Take my ribbon, and hear my prayer. Give me back my father, keep him from the trampling army of the English!"

She stared up at the face of the saint, but still he did not move, so she laid the ribbon hopelessly across his painted wooden foot where it showed beneath his painted wooden gown, and then ran out of the chapel, and along the bridge to the end, through the arched chatelet, past the old Palace of the Bishops, up the hill to the entrance of the new Palace of the Pope, looming high and wide in its mass of dark stone wall.

Soldiers stood on guard there, their tall pikes pointed with bright steel. Jehanne looked at these with the critical eye of an ironwright's daughter, and decided that they were good work—good enough for her father to have made. She proceeded confidently toward them. One of the soldiers stopped her by thrusting his pikestaff across her path.

"Now, by Our Lady," he cried, "where go you so fast, little maid? You march like a company of men-at-arms toward a good meal. Have you some great one's permission to enter here?"

Jehanne stared at him. So she could not even enter through the gate? She might have known that. But somehow she was not afraid. "I come to speak with my uncle," she said, "and he is a painter, one of those employed by Master Giovannetti, at work upon the holy prophets that line the great Hall of Audience."

"So," said the pikeman. "And which of these painters of prophets is your uncle?"

"Jehan le Clerc," she answered, simply. "And my name is Jehanne Paesse, of Villeneuve."

"And named for your uncle, little Jehanne?"

"No," she answered, proudly, "but for the Lady of Avignon, the Queen Jehanne of Naples and Countess of Provence, liege of the Emperor."

The pikeman laughed. "Treason!" he cried. "Treason in Villeneuve! You say that too proudly for a bourgeoise of the King of France. And you bear the name of the Queen of Naples? Never tell it aloud in Villeneuve, or the King's soldiers will eat you."

Tears sprang to her eyes with terror. "Those King's soldiers!" she cried. "Oh, what will they not do? First they will take my father, and then they will eat me because I am named for a beautiful queen. And I was named for her because then we dwelt in Avignon, and we also belonged to the Empire, and enjoyed the peace of the Pope's residence. But the rent was too high here," she finished, suddenly.

The second soldier laughed. "Let no man frighten you," he said, gently. "The King of France cares nothing if your name be Beelzebub, or even Mahomet. There is a page boy watching a dice game inside the guardroom. He will take you to your uncle if you ask him prettily. There are ten pages here to each errand and they grow too fat with idleness." He called through a narrow window to the right of the portal.

"Holà, Carl the German, here is heavy labor for you! Square your shoulders, throw up your chin, and conduct this maid with due ceremony to her uncle, a painter named Jehan le Clerc. He is reputed to be painting prophets in the Hall of Audience. If he is elsewhere no doubt you can find him. And, Carl, do not eat the child, though you grow thin with hunger. She is a vassal of the King of France, and he will wage war on your Emperor if you do. Then the poor King will have the English o' one side of him, and the Germans o' the other. A proper plight for any king, say I!"

The page Carl was very round and fat. He had straight pale hair, and small bright-blue eyes. His tunic was of faded blue velvet, and his long hosen were rose-colored and also faded. His shoes were narrow and pointed and of such a length in the toes that he had tied them by a ribbon to his knees. They were the only new part of his attire. Jehanne stared at them, puzzled. She had never seen shoes like that. The boy strutted a little, proud to seem so friendly with the guardsmen, for the Pope's livery was even more important than his own illustrious master's.

"Come, Jehanne," he cried, "and though 'tis true I am often hungry, I promise I won't eat you this day!"

The guardsmen laughed loud at Carl's admission that he was often hungry, but Jehanne answered him stoutly: "Small good it would do you to eat me, for I am sure His Holiness the Pope would not allow an ogre in his palace. He would send you home to eat visitors to the Palace of the Emperor."

The guardsmen laughed again. "She had you there, hungry Carl," said the first.

Carl tried to make an answer, but he always thought of answers too late. So, he led Jehanne through the great gate, then turned sharp to the right along the wall, and so to the other side of the courtyard, to a tall new building, as high as six stories of the towers. It had tall pointed windows in two rows. She gasped at its huge magnificence, and was a little frightened at the number of people around her. Monks and priests, ladies and waiting women, serving men, pages, soldiers, nobles—a hurrying great crowd seemed to inhabit that court, all brightly dressed, all eager. She slipped her hand into that of Carl, and walked so with him, dazzled by the strange sights around her, and afraid to miss any of them.

They entered a tall doorway, and descended a short,

rounded flight of steps into a huge, long room, supported in
the center by a line of heavy stone pillars finely wrought.
The walls were covered with white plaster, on which were
begun the paintings of a row of prophets. Jehanne would

THE GREAT AUDIENCE HALL.

have stopped to stare at them, for she had never seen so much
to interest her before—a blur of brightness, a procession of
tall figures, each more beautiful than the last. How wonderful to be a painter, she thought, how much better than to be
an ironwright like her father!

"This is the Audience Hall," said Carl, "and your uncle

is yonder in the blue blouse, grinding red color. He is making the pattern of Solomon's robe."

Jehanne stared. "Uncle Jehan!" she cried. "Oh, Uncle Jehan!"

"What brings you here?" he asked, surprised, for the workmen had few visitors while at work, and never before had Jehanne come all the way from Villeneuve.

But Jehanne was too full of interest to answer. She was staring down at the white eggshells under the bench. "Eggs!" she cried. "Do you eat eggs while you work?"

"We must have something to make the color stick to the wall," he answered, "and what could be more natural than eggs? Sometimes the whites, sometimes the yellows, but eggs always. Did you come from Villeneuve to find that out, little Jehanne?"

Slowly she shook her head, and the tears came into her eyes. She had forgotten her errand for a few moments. "Oh, no, Uncle!" she cried. "Oh, no, not for that! Only there was so much to see for the first time—it is my father. The King of France makes war upon the English, far away to the north, but he has sent for my father to help him, and if my father goes Benezet must find another master, and there will be no one to forge the iron, and we shall starve, because he has spent all our money for the house and the iron for a great gate that is but half finished, and no one will pay money for half a gate. Oh, Uncle Jehan, will you not ask your master, our lord the Pope, to intercede for us? He could ask the

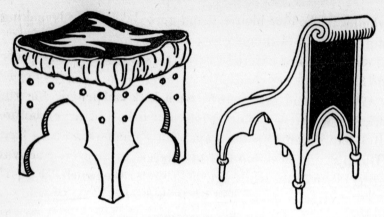

CHAIRS FROM THE POPE'S PALACE.

King to let my father stay, and surely the King would do it if the Pope asked him."

"Surely indeed," said Jehan le Clerc. "But who am I, to make such a request of His Holiness? This is no injustice, little maid, but your father's duty to his liege lord, and he is but one among thousands. The poor must obey. That is the law of our life. And only twice since I have worked here have I seen His Holiness. Each time he came we knelt at his approach, and scarcely dared to raise our eyes lest he think us lacking in respect. Never would I dare to speak to him. If I were not struck dumb for my brazenness I should surely be thrown out of the palace, and forced to seek employment elsewhere. And then you would be worse off than before, for I could not give you what little help I now can. Not a great deal, child, not enough to keep you, but what I can, I will, and pray the saints to send more. If you were but a little older we might find you a place in one of the great houses, but since you are not yet twelve, they would not take you. And you the oldest child! A sad thing. You must card wool for spinning, and your mother must weave. Perhaps you can spin, too. It will not bring much, but it will have to answer. How else can a woman with five children earn money to feed them?"

"And what of my father?" she sobbed. "Suppose I do card wool and spin, and so gain a few pennies of good red copper, will that protect my father? What of him? Oh, Uncle Jehan, you must do something! If only he could stay, then all were well again."

"If you had but remained in Avignon all would now be well. The Queen of Naples, our liege lady, is at war with

A FOLDING STOOL.

the King of Hungary, but she will levy no soldiers from the Pope's city, through respect for him."

" 'Tis too late to move back," she moaned. "The soldiers of the King have come already. Think you they would seek my father here if he took refuge in Avignon?"

"Assuredly," answered her uncle. "If he were some great lord the Pope would give him protection, but to a humble master workman, and he with but one poor apprentice—no, Jehanne, there is no way but to go and fight the English."

Jehanne sobbed into his shoulder. Her journey had been a failure. St. Nicholas had not cared for a red ribbon. Even the saints, and such a saint as the kindly Nicholas, who brought gifts freely to all good children on the eve of his festival, would not help her. For the first time in her life she knew that the world was indeed hard for the poor, and she felt more desolate than she had known was possible. Jehan tried to comfort her, whispering in her ear, but she could not stop her sobs. They were thick and heavy in her throat, and would not be silenced. Her uncle's voice grew more insistent, but she could not hear what he was saying. The words meant nothing. St. Nicholas had failed her, and her father must go away to fight against strange, wicked, fierce English soldiers, who would thrust pikes at him—pikes like those the guard at the gate held. She felt her uncle drop to his knees from the bench where he had been sitting, felt him push her so that she too knelt on the stone floor, and still the sobs would not cease, still she murmured over and over:

"St. Nicholas, oh, St. Nicholas, help me, St. Nicholas,

help my father! Oh, St. Nicholas, you will not desert me, dear St. Nicholas, only you, only you can help me now!"

Arms were around her, she felt herself gathered against the breast of some man who was not Uncle Jehan, a breast hard and sharp with jewels, and above it was a chin shaven smooth, and the hands that held her were heavy with rings. She gasped a little in terror—had the saint himself come to answer her? She stared up, her sobs stopped by the thought, and saw a small white cap upon hair dark but with a little gray in it, a face with kindly eyes and a wide mouth drawn into a gentle, pitying smile, and a voice was speaking to her.

"What do you ask of the saint?" the voice asked, tenderly.

"Oh, holy St. Nicholas," she whispered, "I pray your pardon! You who have so high a seat in Heaven, and such great affairs, I beg pardon. Good St. Nicholas, who am I to ask your aid? But, oh, kind St. Nicholas, help my father, please! The King of France can surely spare him from his great army, when he has so many, and we need him so. The gate is but half done, you see, and no one will pay for a gate half finished. Surely even a saint can understand that much of ironwork. Don't let him go away to fight the English, good St. Nicholas. You can stop him. Oh, you have answered my prayer, and it is a miracle, and you will stop him, surely!"

She had slipped down and was kneeling at his feet, clasping his knees in her thin arms, staring up at his face in awe and hope and a little terror.

The tender voice answered: "I am not St. Nicholas, though it may be that he sent me to you. Certainly I had no intention of coming to see the painting when I went to rest last night. I thought I came because it was such a fine morning, but perhaps the saint willed it. Have no fear. Your

"I AM CLEMENT THE POPE."

father shall not go to war against the English. If I ask it, the King will not take him. What is his name, little one?"

"Régnier Paesse," she answered, "of Villeneuve—the iron-wright. It is a beautiful gate, my lord. Tell me, who are you, if not St. Nicholas?"

"I am Clement the Pope," the man answered, and Jehanne

caught her breath, and dropped her eyes in shame at her boldness.

"Oh, Holy Father, forgive me!" she whispered. "I would not have dared to ask you if I had known."

"As well you did not know," he answered, smiling. "But you would dare to ask a saint and not a man?"

"Not you," she said. "You are greater than the King, and I would not dare to ask the King. But a saint, and especially such a one as kind St. Nicholas, why, Holy Father, a saint's business is to help poor folk, is it not? They delight in prayers, and such we may give them. I laid my new red ribbon at his feet, and in return he sent you to help me. When I cross the bridge again I will give him thanks. If I had aught else I would leave it also at his feet, but the ribbon was all I had fine enough to offer to a saint."

The Pope held out his hand to her. "You may kiss the ring," he said, graciously, "as kings and princes do." Fearfully she touched her lips to its bright jewel, wondering if it would burn her. It felt a little cool, and hard, like any ring, and while she was wondering why it should not be hot with holiness, Clement put into her hand a carved gold cross, on a chain of twisted links, curiously wrought.

"I give you this," he said. "It is worth more than your father with all his labor can earn in a sixmonth. It is yours, to keep or give away as you see fit. But as you pass the bridge again, do not fail to thank St. Nicholas, for surely your father shall stay with you, Jehanne. And for your sake I will also commission him to forge some ironwork for the palace. Go in peace with my blessing, little daughter!"

"Kiss his slipper, kiss his slipper!" whispered her uncle quickly, and she leaned forward to touch her lips to the gold embroidered cross that even kings must kiss, and few maids of her station were permitted ever to approach.

Then Clement the Pope passed on to speak with Master Giovannetti, who remained on his knees, and Carl the German took her by the hand, and led her quickly out into the courtyard again.

"When the Holy Father came in," he said, "I thought the lightning would strike you down, and 'twas the nearest to a miracle I shall ever see. Never will I forget this day, Jehanne."

"Nor I!" she cried. "But why should the lightning strike me, Carl? Is the Holy Father, then, so fierce?"

"Not fierce, but full of majesty, and far above little, crying maids. Even I, though in his service—at least, indirectly, serving one who serves him—have never seen him before this day. So frightened I was, I was like to fall through into the cellar below or to fly upward into the great chapel—only I have no wings. And you with your St. Nicholas! How you dared!"

But Jehanne wasn't listening. She had seen the gate ahead, and she dropped Carl's hand, no longer interested in the courtyard and its hurrying crowds, but as swift as any rabbit she ran through the gate and down the street, toward the bridge of St. Benezet and the figure of St. Nicholas.

SHE·RAN·SWIFT·AS·ANY·RABBIT~DOWN·THE·STREET·TOWARD·THE·BRIDGE

The chapel was deserted. She dropped on her knees to say her prayer of thanks, and laid the gold cross on the floor before her. How kind he had been to her! She stared at the gold, forgetting to pray. A jewel to grace even such a saint, who did not scorn a simple maid. She sprang up suddenly, her eyes shining, and climbed upon the altar, where she reached up as high as might be to place the chain around the hard wooden neck of the saint. She fastened it securely, for it was too fine to risk its falling off and she was not sure she would ever dare approach so near to put it on again.

When she had finished she climbed down and knelt to say a prayer to mitigate her boldness for touching the figure. She stared up now at the bright cross with admiration and thankfulness. Surely he had never had a finer gift than that? Surely he was smiling at her just a little? He was pleased. She sighed.

"Blessed, holy St. Nicholas," she said, "I give you all my thanks. Perhaps now you have finished with the red ribbon? The cross is so fine you would surely not notice a little ribbon? Perhaps I might take it back again, since you have the other. His Holiness said the cross is worth more than my father earns in a sixmonth. Surely you would not be offended. What would so great a saint do with a little red ribbon?"

She reached forward and touched the ribbon, watching the saint's face as she did so, and she thought he nodded to her, so she took the ribbon, and tied it on her dress again, and then went out into the warm sunlight, and took her way happily back across the bridge toward the little house outside the walls of Villeneuve.

Thus Régnier Paesse finished his gate, and Jehan le Clerc finished painting the pattern on the robe of Solomon. You can see them both if you go to Avignon to look for them.

SOLOMON IN HIS ROBE.

Popes and Nobles

By far the nicest way to approach Avignon is by boat, and if you should take that way, you would be borne swiftly down the Rhone on its strong current, while the boatmen, as they steered their craft, would still use the old words "Realm" for the right bank, and "Empire" for the left bank, though both have belonged to the Republic of France for more than a hundred years.

You would see first a few arches of the bridge of St. Benezet, with the little chapel of St. Nicholas on its second pier, and you would know at once that this was Avignon. Next the city walls would loom, with their battlements of stone, called "machicoulis," and you would know by that that these walls are much newer than those of Carcassonne, where the battlements were made of wood. That does not prove that Avignon is a younger city than Carcassonne, for

HELENE GARTER

THE · PALACE · OF · THE · POPES · AT · THE · TIME · OF · CLEMENT VI

there used to be an inner line of walls, much smaller than these and now torn down. The old walls were much too small to protect a city that had become the center of the Christian world, so Pope Clement started building these new ones.

Almost at the same time you first see the battlements of Avignon, you will also see the cathedral on its high rock. Let us forget it now, because it has been rebuilt and is very ugly, and look just beyond it to see, quite close and very majestic and lovely, full of dreams and ghosts of its own, the Palace of the Popes. In the time of Jehanne it was called the strongest and most beautiful fortress in Christendom. Now it looks from the outside like a rugged mass of gray stonework, a little gloomy and very shabby. But inside, many of its rooms are bright with fresco paintings of saints and prophets, of hunting scenes with unicorns and some less imaginary animals, and of bright birds in the tops of trees full of fruit.

The whole pile is a series of towers, and, like those at Carcassonne, each one has a name and a story of its own. Once inside the gate—the same through which Jehanne went —you will not be much reminded of this machine century in which we live, for Avignon is a quiet place to-day, and of all its greatness only memories are left. Some of the streets are narrow and winding as they were when cardinals and great nobles lived behind the dull-gray stone fronts of the houses lining them. There are pretty gardens back of some of the houses and in the Street of the Dyers you will find a stream with tiny bridges across it from house to house, and great

water wheels at intervals, to keep the water fresh and
moving.

If you want to go out on the bridge of St. Benezet you will
have to go through a house whose owner would probably
rather not be disturbed at her housework. If you persuade
her to let you, you can go into the same little chapel where
Jehanne laid her ribbon at the feet of St. Nicholas. You will
have to enter by a different door from the one Jehanne used,
because the old roadway of the bridge has been raised to the
highest level of the arches, and the old entrance to the chapel
closed up by the masonry. A narrow flight of stairs had to
be built over the side of the bridge, with a new door in the
wall of the little building. If you have a red ribbon, you can
lay it at the saint's feet, and thank him for your last Christmas gifts, for he is the same St. Nicholas we call "Santa
Claus." You can see how he changed his name if you
pronounce it as they did in the northern countries, "Sant
Ni-claws." Say it fast, and it becomes "Santa Claus."

Jehanne, of course, approached the chapel from the Villeneuve side, through the great gateway of the Tower of
Philip the Fair. She lived just outside the southern walls of
Villeneuve. Some very old houses are still standing that she
must have passed on her way to see Pope Clement. The old
Fort of St. André is there now, and much as it always was.
If you climb up inside the Tower of Philip, in the very top
room you will find a chessboard cut into the stone floor. It
was probably made by some prisoners, who may have

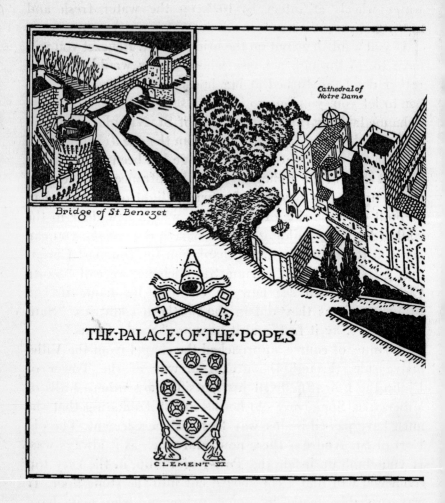

Bridge of St Benezet

Cathedral of Notre Dame

THE·PALACE·OF·THE·POPES

CLEMENT VI

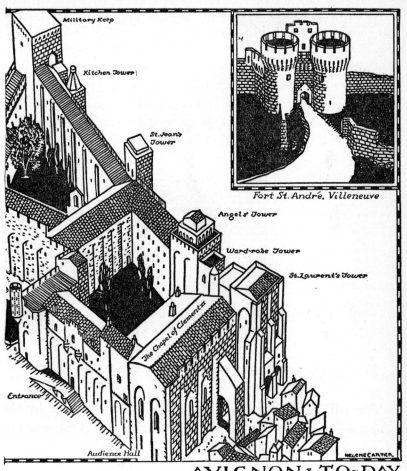

Military Keep

Kitchen Tower

St. Jean's Tower

Angels' Tower

Ward-robe Tower

St. Laurent's Tower

The Chapel of Clementz

Entrance

Audience Hall

HELENE CARTER

Fort St. André, Villeneuve

AVIGNON · TO·DAY

watched Jehanne as she crossed the bridge. Between games of chess they would have had nothing else to do but watch the people on the bridge.

THE NORTH GATEWAY TO THE POPE'S PALACE.

You will have to go to Villeneuve in your boat, or by the new bridge across the Rhone to the south of Avignon, but except for the short crossing of the river you can take every step of Jehanne's trip as she did and see almost exactly what she saw on the way. So many of the old buildings are still there, a little grayer, a little softer on the edges than they were, but Jehanne would recognize them if she could come back to them.

A SOLDIER WITH A CROSSBOW.

When you leave the bridge of St. Benezet, after thanking St. Nicholas for your roller skates and the Christmas tree— or was it a sled and some books?—you will have to tilt your head backward a little to see the Palace of the Popes on its rocky hill. It seems high even to us, used as we are to tall buildings. Jehanne's gateway is open, though its guardian is no longer a soldier of the Pope. He will tell you to turn to the left to go to the Audience Hall. Jehanne made the same turn at just the same sharp angle, passed through the same courtyard, and entered the same passageway, and the Audience Hall looks to-day much as it did then, for when Jehanne saw it, it was not yet quite finished—the heads had not been painted on the Prophets that line its walls. Since that time some poor soldiers who did not know any better have cut out the heads and sold them, so that you will see headless prophets as Jehanne did, with their robes bright against the gray stone walls where the plaster has fallen away.

Let us hope the soldiers spent the money they received for the heads dancing on the bridge to the old tune. Do you remember it?

> *"Sur le pont d'Avignon*
> *L'on y danse, l'on y danse,*
> *Sur le pont d'Avignon*
> *L'on y danse, tout en rond."*

> "On the bridge of Avignon,
> Everybody dances, dances,
> On the bridge of Avignon,
> Dances, dances, round and round."

But probably they bought cakes and sweetmeats with the money. The bridge was already broken, and Avignon dancing was done indoors by them.

Having satisfied yourself with the sight of Solomon's bright-spotted robe in the Audience Hall, you can climb up a

narrow stairway wound into the wall like those in the towers
at Carcassonne, to the chapel above it. Pope Clement was
very proud of this chapel, and waited impatiently for it to
be finished. He held only one service in it before he died,
having done more for the city of Avignon than any other
person.

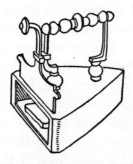

THIS IRON MAY HAVE PRESSED CLEMENT'S ROBES.

He made his home in the Tower of the Angels. You can
see the room where he slept, the room where he kept his
clothes in the Wardrobe Tower, the offices where his secre-
taries worked, the kitchens where his food was cooked, the
little back door where the groceries were delivered. Or if
you can't go to Avignon to see these things in plaster and
stone and paint, you can see them in the pictures in this book,
the way they were as well as the way they are now. And if
cooking food in kitchens does not sound as interesting as the
rest, remember that people had learned to build their fires

at the side of their rooms, with a chimney to carry off the smoke, but Pope Clement's cooking fire was built in the center of the room, with a huge eight-sided chimney like a hollow pyramid above, rising through the roof so high that half of Avignon can see it. It allowed the cooking to be done on all sides of the fire, instead of on one side only, and that must have been necessary, for Clement had so many visitors that at times he had to put beds along the walls of all the public rooms in his palace to give them shelter. Feeding them must have taxed the resources of even such a kitchen as this. There is another kitchen built like Pope Clement's, in the royal palace at Cintra, Portugal. It may have been copied from the one at Avignon. There were a great many Portuguese visitors at Avignon to take the idea back with them.

Perhaps we should explain why the popes built a palace at Avignon. They had always lived at Rome, but in the fourteenth century Italy was so very much troubled by wars that they found it unsafe, and so for seventy years they made their home beside the Rhone. To them, of course, came ambassadors from the rulers of all nations, even from some who were not Christian, such as the Khan of Tartary. The city quickly became rich and fashionable, and the court was the center of learning and luxury.

Pope Clement, who gave the cross and chain to Jehanne, built most of the palace. He was a Frenchman, a very kindly person, fond of bright colors and fine clothes and tall buildings and good books. He was always glad to see people

CASTLES·HAD·GROWN·TO·THREE·TIMES·THE·SIZE.

THE *HOURDES* OF PEPIN'S TIME HAD CHANGED TO STONE.

happy, and disliked wars, but he built his palace strong enough to resist a siege. Then he started new and strong walls large enough to surround the city, so that he really lived in a fortress within a fortress, like the castle within the walls of Carcassonne. But do not imagine that it was a gloomy place. It seems so, now, with its bright rugs and hangings gone, but people had grown to love gayety, castles had grown to three times the size they were of old, and they were more fancifully built, more comfortable, and had larger openings for windows. The last would not have been much of an advantage if people had not learned to make better glass, and to fill their windows with it. That, of course, kept out the cold, so that the openings no longer deserved the name we still give them of "wind-ows."

Glass has been made for thousands of years. To-day it is

made for windows in large flat sheets, very clear and almost without color. In Pepin's day it was made in flat slides, uneven and narrow, full of little bubbles, and greenish or lavenderish in hue even when not deliberately colored. The slides were expensive, but occasionally some one made a window of them, laid like clapboards, one above the other. They shed rain and let in light, but left cracks for wind. The glass that Pope Clement put in the windows of his chapel was first blown into great bubbles, then small pieces were cut from the bubbles and joined by soft binders of lead, to make large, flat, air-tight panes. The bubbles could be brightly colored. By using bits from different bubbles a lot of small pieces would make patterns and figures, so that the finest windows became great pictures in brilliant, glowing color.

As soon as people made windows larger they could see their rooms better, and then they wanted to make them more beautiful. They painted their furniture in bright designs, or covered it with woven and embroidered stuffs, and when they did not have the walls of their rooms painted with pictures, they hung them with more stuffs, and gradually these became more magnificent. The first of the popes of Avignon draped his personal apartments with simple dark-green serge. The next was more luxurious; he had red and blue taffeta. But Clement, Jehanne's friend, hung his walls with marvelous weavings from Damascus, with Arabic texts in gold thread declaring Mahomet to be the Prophet of Allah! He might have been a little surprised if he, the head of the Christian Church, could have read them.

Clement even put rugs on his floors. That was quite a new idea. Before his day people had brought rugs from the East, but had laid them under a throne, as a decoration, or hung them on walls. Walking on them was considered a great extravagance. The first popes had been content with mats of

AN ANIMAL CANDLESTICK.

braided straw, rushes, or strewn lavender-twigs to keep their feet from the cold stone. Clement bought almost numberless Oriental rugs. Some of them were Moorish from Spain, some Turkish, some had the Pope's coat of arms woven on them to order. He also used some cheaper rugs of European velvet. The one under his throne in the great Audience Hall was decorated with green parroquets and white swans.

Clement the Pope, like most of the great nobles of his

time, was fond of seeing his coat of arms. He had it carved and painted on the ceilings of the rooms he built, between the dove of his office and the arms of Rome. It is there now, over and over again, a reminder of a great man's great place in the world. He also put it on chairs, on chests, and had it

COSTUMES OF POPE CLEMENT'S TIME.

embroidered on his retainers' clothing, though of course we cannot see those any longer.

Clement wasn't the only person who dressed his servants in livery. The habit started in the Middle Ages. The word in French is *livrée*, which means "delivered." They were called so because it was the custom for a lord to deliver clothes to all the people of his household on certain holidays. "People" in this case meant his family, too—every one on his estates except the *vilains*, who were not villains, but farm workers. They were seldom remembered at all unless they did not pay their rents, and then they wished to be forgotten. Naturally, the closest relatives got the prettiest materials and colors, but noble or simple, they all bore brightly across the front of their outer garments the arms of their lord. This was very useful, because it made it easy to distinguish the people of one great family from another, especially in a crowded city of strangers like Avignon, where every lord was jealous of every other lord. They all liked a good deal of casual fighting, and the *livrées* saved many a friend from having a stone hurled at him in mistake for an enemy.

People in those days thought fighting the most noble and honorable of occupations. The peaceful arts were looked upon as fit only for monks, women, and the lower classes, while strong men of noble birth occupied their time either starting wars or building battlements to defend themselves in case some one else started one first. Sometimes they also built churches in the hope that they would be forgiven for the wars.

And yet, while all this fighting was using up such a lot of time and energy, there seem to have been enough peaceful people to do more important things. Professions came into fashion. Universities grew out of small groups of students. People learned to read and write, and there were even trained lawyers and scribes who were not monks, but Masters of Arts, though most of these accepted some church appoint-

ment after the fashion of the time. Petrarch was such a
Master of Arts, and he lived for a long time in Avignon,
where he met his lovely Laura. He was a very great poet,
and his love story has been written a hundred times since his
day, but he left another reminder of himself that is in con-
stant use. In an age when all books were copied by hand, a
scholar's penmanship was very important. Petrarch's was so
delicate and exact that on it, it is said, the "Italic" characters
are modeled, though we spell the word with a small *i* now.
Much of his writing was done at Avignon, where he was a
member of the Pope's court. He must have crossed the bridge
of St. Benezet a thousand times, and wandered in and out of
the great palace day after day.

Though more people could read in Petrarch's time than in
that of our Frankish ghost, education and books were still
very expensive and scholars had a hard time, unless they

were lucky enough to be given some church position. Their other chief means of livelihood was copying manuscripts. Printing was not yet thought of, and books were not published, but merely written down. When a man had finished

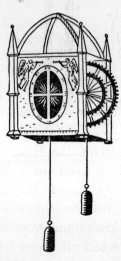

A CLOCK RUN BY COUNTERWEIGHTS.

a new poem or tale or history, he presented it to some great lord, and hoped to receive a present for it. There was no rule about such presents, and if the lord gave too little there was nothing the poor author could do about it except offer his next book to some one else. A great many writers chose to present their books to Pope Clement, because he was rich and generous, though he must have been so very busy that he had little time for reading.

In the days of Euric time was kept in the churches, by
means of wax candles that burned a certain distance in an
hour, and after each candle the bell was rung, to let the
people know the time. They also had sandglasses like our
kitchen eggtimers, but Pope Clement's engagements were
kept exact by means of a clock run by counterweights, just
like a cuckoo clock without the cuckoo. It had to be hung on
the wall so that the weights could move up and down freely.
Such clocks were still a valuable novelty, and even the Pope
could not have one in every room. The cook used a sandglass
to time his roasts and eggs, and listened for the church bell
to know when to begin. The other members of the household
either deciphered the intricate markings of a sundial, or
sent a page to the clock to see if it were time to dress for
dinner.

And dinner was still at the old time, ten in the morning.
When Petrarch was asked to dine at the Pope's table he
would see Clement use a fork. Most people of the time had
never heard of such an instrument. They still ate their food
with fingers or spoons, and forks were at first thought very
silly and fussy. Pope Clement used them only for eating
fruit, which he apparently found more difficult to eat tidily
with the fingers than meat and vegetables. It should be
explained that the people of some countries still use fingers
instead of forks, and manage very neatly—much better than
we should do without practice.

Pope Clement kept his fork with his table knife and spoon,
in a "boat" of carved and enameled silver. So that no one

could touch the implements between meals, it had a lock and key and stood before his place at the table, on a cloth of fine linen, beside a saltcellar of gold set with precious stones. There was nothing else on the table when he and his guests

A MONOCORD.

sat down to their meal. Everything was passed to them by men of knightly birth, proud of the honor of serving so exalted a personage. After the meal was finished, a silver basin with a pitcher of water and a napkin were passed so that the company might wash and dry their hands. Those who were not honored by being asked to sit at the private table of the Pope had to go to the side of the room to wash at a "fountain." That was a tank filled with water, with a basin below it. It had a faucet that could be turned on and off, and a railing to hold the napkin. The men-at-arms ate from the cooking-pot, and licked their fingers as clean as they could.

A HORSE LITTER FOR TRAVELING.

Probably the fork that Pope Clement used was a present from somebody, for nobody had more presents than he. Kings and princes vied with each other to see which could give him the most interesting, new, and expensive things, and then they traveled to Avignon to see each other's gifts, and have them copied for themselves. Copying taught the workmen of Europe their finest trades.

Everyone traveled, though the roads were terrible. No one bothered to mend them, so that they were thick with dust or deep in mud most of the time. Avignon had more visitors than any other city, and because of the state of the roads most people came on horseback, or by horse litter. Here is a picture of a litter. It looks very comfortable, doesn't it? Of course there were carriages, too, made very gay with painting, but as a rule, they were not used very far from cities, because they were so likely to stick in the mud. Merchants traveled from castle to castle and city to city, carrying their goods on donkeyback and trying to look as poor as possible so that robbers should not molest them. It all sounds very slow to us, with our fast cars and railroads, yet the messengers of the great could cover the distance between Paris and Avignon in five days. That is about four hundred miles, and must have required hard riding. No doubt the men who did it were glad indeed to come within sight of the battlements of Avignon, where they could rest and refresh themselves under the bright sun of Provence, beside the swift-flowing Rhone, and listen to the boatmen calling to each other, "Realm!" or "Empire!" while the Pope, as liege lord of the Christian Church, ruled over both.

MONT SAINT-MICHEL

THE BATTLEMENTS OF THE MONKS

Accolade

COLETTE TABARY uttered a delighted cry when she saw the towers of Mont Saint-Michel rising through the dusk of early dawn. She and André were almost at the shore's edge before the fog parted and showed the top of the tall pyramid. Stage on stage it rose from the flat white sands, half natural rock, half man-made walls and spires. As they rode nearer, the rising sun fell across its highest reaches and bathed it in fairy light, making each pinnacle show more sharply against the soft gray of the misty early sky. André nodded toward it.

" 'Tis a fine sight in the dawn," he said. "St. Michael loves high places, and that seems doubly high, rising so sharply from the sands. They say when the good St. Aubert wished to build the first church, St. Michael had to work a miracle before the peak was leveled enough."

"St. Michael still works miracles," Colette said piously. "Many seek protection of him, and last year 'tis said a young maid was cured of a shaking sickness by water brought from the mount."

"Perhaps he will work a miracle to aid me," André said softly.

"What miracle have you need of?" Colette asked. "You have no trembling sickness, nor do you need protection, a strong lad like you with your great dog always near."

" 'Tis not protection I ask, but aid," he answered, "and I have a most mortal sickness, though I would not be cured. 'Tis another thing I would ask of the sainted archangel."

Colette looked at him and laughed. "Never," said she, "have I seen a youth with less appearance of mortal hurt than you. How does this great hurt harm you?"

"It does not harm me," answered André. "It is a most happy hurt, but mortal, for all that. I'm like to die of it, any moment."

"What nonsense you talk!" She laughed gayly. "Explain your riddle, then."

" 'Tis a riddle of love," he answered.

"Oh!" she said, tossing her dark head in its tight velvet hood. "And is the maid of your choice beautiful?"

"Very," he answered.

"Is she gentle?"

"By disposition."

"I meant by birth. Is she far?"

"Too far for me to reach, but near enough to see and serve."

MONT·SAINT·MICHEL ∼ IN·PERIL·OF·THE·SEA·

Colette laughed again, teasingly. " 'Tis a very difficult riddle," she said quickly. "Does she return your admiration?"

"Ah, that," said André, "I have not been able to discover. I have given her every chance to tell me, but she only asks questions whose answers she knows."

" 'Tis a way of maids," said Colette. "They wish to hear their beauty praised plain—and often."

"I have told her plain enough," said André, "so that she may understand, and as often as I dared. More plainly I must not speak till her father or the King give me leave."

"And when think you that will be?" she asked.

"I hope it may be after I have made my prayers to the archangel on his chosen mount, if the holy St. Michael will stoop from his high place to work a miracle for me."

"Is so small a thing a miracle?" she asked.

"No less," he answered. "What am I? A penniless bourgeois lad, a humble clerk of Master Tabary, and the maid's father rightly plans a knightly match for her. What hope have I to gain the accolade? And even that were scarce enough. She should become a duchess at the least. No less a title were good enough for her."

"Perhaps," said Colette, "you think her fairer than she is. She may have seen no dukes good enough. They are all bald or fat. If perchance you should become a knight, it would not surprise me greatly if her father consented to the match. He—that is—*my* father—esteems you greatly."

André looked at her and shook his head. "That may be

true enough," he said, sadly, "but how can I hope for the King's accolade—I, a poor clerk, without noble friends to recommend me?"

"Our good King Louis XI—may the saints preserve him!" said Colette, "is no respecter of nobles. Look around you. Here, in this train, are two bourgeois to each noble, and since the maid of your choice is herself of humble birth, why should she look so high?"

"Her father looks for her," answered André. "And though the King surrounds himself with commoners, he does not make them knights. I put my faith in the holy St. Michael. Only by a miracle can I hope to wed my chosen maid."

"You need not make the miracle too hard to perform," she suggested, practically. "Call it what you will, but if between your prayers you keep close to the King, it may be you will find some service to offer, and he may reward you for it."

André laughed. "That would be good advice," he said, "if I had not followed it steadfastly for months already. The King has so many courtiers I never get close enough to him to do him any service. Who am I to serve a king?"

"A loyal lad with a strong arm and a brave heart," she answered. "Prayer to the archangel is pious and good, but a quick wit is not to be despised." She laughed and rode away from him toward the group ahead.

The occasion of the journey was a pilgrimage by the King to see the new buildings finished within the year by his old friend and loyal supporter, Guillaume d'Estouteville, Abbot

of the Monastery of St. Michael. The Abbot now appeared
on the road ahead, with two monks and twenty knights,
coming to greet his King. The sun was just over the eastern
horizon. Word had come the night before that they must
start early, because only at low tide could horsemen ride
across the white sands. At high tide the mount could be
approached by boat, but at half-tide the waters rushed too
swiftly, and no one came or went. All the men except the
King dismounted as the Abbot came abreast. He and his
knights knelt to welcome their royal visitor, and the King
was gracious to them, and bade them rise and mount again.

"If it please your Majesty," said the Abbot, " 'twould be
as well to proceed quickly, for the tide has already turned,
and it will come so swift no horse can outrace it."

The King shuddered as he looked out across the wide
reach of white sands, flat and dazzling to the eye, with a thin
black line in the distance, that was the sea. "I have heard that
tale," he said, "and I shall be glad to see this sight."

"That you shall, and soon, Sire," answered the Abbot.

"Come quickly, then," said the King nervously. "I prefer
to see this tiderace from the safety of the rock. I would we
were there."

"The mists are gone, Sire," said Master Tabary, riding
beside him. " 'Tis a fine day after all."

"A good omen," answered the King, "for my petition to
the saint. A lordly saint like the holy Archangel Michael
should surely grant the petition of a king, should he not, my
lord Abbot?"

"That were gracious, surely," answered the Abbot politely. "May a humble subject ask the nature of your Majesty's petition?"

"St. Michael is the champion of the brave," answered the King reverently, "and I have many noble men and learned men surrounding me, some of whom are brave and some true, but few of whom are both. I shall ask the saint to show me which can be trusted. I have need of long devotion and of much bravery if our fair land of France is ever to become peaceful and prosperous, as I would see it."

"Perchance," said the Abbot, "the good saint will find it possible to show your Majesty where one such may be found."

"One would be a small showing for so great a saint," answered the King gloomily. "I have come a long way, and 'tis not well for a saint to gain the repute of niggardliness."

"Nor," said Master Tabary dryly, with the friendly freedom of an old and trusted officer of the royal household, "for a king, Sire."

The Abbot smiled decorously behind his hand, remembering Louis' reputation for miserliness. Louis asked: "If the King listened to all the counsel he received to spend and spend and spend, where, think you, would the finances of this land be?"

"And where," answered Master Tabary soberly, "if your officers did not urge spending upon your Majesty, would the army be now? In their homes, or fighting for gain under the banner of the Duke of Burgundy, instead of under your Majesty's standard, the bright oriflamme of St. Denis."

"Let us think of pleasant things," Louis grumbled crossly, "not of my rebellious cousin of Burgundy."

They were close to the mount by then, and its tall mass rose above them in a straight pyramid that seemed to pierce the sky. Almost on a level with the white sands began the first wall of the fortifications, solidly flanked by towers. The great crenelated battlements had defended it well against the English forty years ago, in the unhappy days before the maid Jeanne d'Arc of the village of Domrémy broke their power, so that they went back across the channel to their own island country. King Louis thought of that maid now. St. Michael had been one of her angel counselors. He crossed himself and bowed his head as he remembered.

Behind the outer wall rose steeply, one above the other, the houses of the town, where pilgrims lodged, and above the houses the Abbey fortress, called the "Merveille"—the "Marvel"—crowned by its spired church. As they neared it, from the gateway men's voices rose in a chant of praise and welcome. Velvets, rugs, bright cloaks, strips of silk, banners, ribbons, and garlands of flowers hung from every loophole and window in the little town. A long line of singing monks stood closely packed down the length of the narrow, steeply mounting street, their voices greeting their king in the Latin language of the Church. A hundred knights were drawn up before them, kneeling in feal homage to their lord, their armor burnished, their plumed helmets doffed, their esquires kneeling close behind.

The King was nodding as though satisfied with the show, but he gave no sign of pleasure at his royal welcome. Rather he seemed to be searching among them for something that might be at fault. His dark clothes showed worn and dusty in the sunlight, shabby by comparison with the knights' brightness. Only his wide golden, jeweled collar marked his dress from that of any humble clerk or merchant. Yet, for all his unpretentious dress, his suspicious eyes, and his tight, ungenerous mouth, there was an air of kingliness about him. André, watching from his distant place in the cortège, felt in that moment that of all men he had seen he would rather trust the fortunes of France to that ungracious, long-nosed man than to any other.

"He reasons better," André decided, "and already he has proved reason a better bulwark than high-sounding words or mere force of arms. I'd serve him if to serve him meant the losing all chance of preferment, instead of gaining it." Softly he whispered the battle cry of France, "God, St. Denis, and King Louis!"

The long cavalcade wound slowly up toward the Abbey. "It has been arranged," said d'Estouteville, "that pilgrimages should cease during your Majesty's visit, to make room for your retainers, and for greater safety. But a few, because of vows they had taken, or because of great need, we have allowed to come."

"A pilgrim's cloak," said the King, "makes an excellent shield for an assassin or a thief."

"They are closely guarded by our men-at-arms," the Abbot assured him, "so that no ill-wisher can approach you, Sire."

The King looked about him as though he half expected to see pilgrims rise from the stones, a knife in the hand of each. Instead he saw a man-at-arms coming toward them. The man spoke to the knights ahead. One of them took from him a paper, and passed it back. The lane was too narrow for the messenger to go with it. The Abbot received it, and offered it to the King.

"A petition, most like. A pilgrim brought it, and swore it was of great and immediate importance."

"Give it to Master Tabary," said Louis, drawing away from the paper as though he feared it might attack him.

Master Tabary broke the seal, and unwrapped the ribbon that bound it. He read:

"My Lord:

"I have followed you to the mount of the Most Holy Archangel, protector of the brave and loyal. If so be it is your royal pleasure to remember a poor woman who did you service when you were a young prince, in refuge at the Court of Burgundy, then, in your puissance, aid my son, Philip. He lies now in peril of death because of a letter of your Majesty's that I had treasured for fifteen years. It bore your thanks to my humble self because I had been able to bring you messages from your friends in France while you were in exile. That letter I gave to my son, that your royal signature might bring him grace, but it bore no date, and now it has been discovered, and because of it my son has been accused of treason by the captains of Burgundy. Only the absence of Duke Charles has saved him so long. There is little time to save him if so be your Majesty will interest your royal self in the cause of one so unworthy. In the name of St. Michael I beseech you, mercy! My devotion to your Majesty, and may the blessings of all the saints and of Our Lady rest upon you and yours!

> "Your servant,
> "Margot Dieudonné."

When Master Tabary had finished reading he folded the letter again, and waited until the cortège had stopped. Then, when all had dismounted and passed within the sheltering shadow of the abbey fortress, he drew near to the King.

"Knew you a woman named Margot Dieudonné?" he asked.

"Margot Dieudonné?" the King repeated. "A common enough name. Where?"

"Fifteen years ago, at the Court of Burgundy."

"Yes," Louis answered, "I remember her. What of her? A good soul, and loyal to me when I had no kingdom."

Master Tabary gave her letter to the King. Louis's thin face grew thinner and his lips tighter as he read. Slowly he nodded and sighed. "A small request to make of a king," he said, sadly, "to rescue one man from my own vassal's hands. A small request, but very difficult to perform. Here is one of those cases where I have need of the brave and trustworthy man I mean to ask the saint to show me."

"Perhaps," suggested Master Tabary, "the saint shows you this Philip Dieudonné—his very name means 'given of God.'"

A WAGON OF LOUIS'S TIME.

"Then," said the King, making a wry face, "he must show me a way to rescue him. No one of my knights or my officers can go to him, for they would be known, and Duke Charles would deal with them as he has with poor Margot's son. Him I remember, too—a bright little lad, with yellow curls. She taught him to call me 'your Majesty.' Some one unknown must go—some one who can travel hard and dare readily, some one with a touch of luckiness. Who is that man, among all this company?"

"Sire," said Master Tabary, "may I suggest one quite unknown, loyal I know, brave I believe, and lucky enough to have won the regard of my Colette?"

"That boy, André? Certainly he's unknown, and lucky indeed if Colette has regard for him." King Louis curled his lip scornfully.

"He's gay and young enough," pursued Master Tabary, "so that no one would suspect him of a serious errand, and Colette has begged a chance for him."

"Colette is a pretty child," Louis answered more graciously, "but is that a reason for trusting the lad? He's a clerk—why should he be brave? I know nothing of his loyalty. No, it must be one better proven than André."

"There is not much time to choose," said Master Tabary. "You were to ask St. Michael to show you a man both brave and loyal. To prove this miracle this man should show himself on the mount. But since the saint may be occupied with other things, and so delay, may I suggest a plan, Sire?"

"Suggest, and be quick," said the King, "but do not ask me to trust to one unproven the rescue of good Margot's brave and loyal son. Philip must be both, for if he had not been he would not have carried my letter with him on Burgundian ground. I have been shown one brave and loyal, in this Philip. But that's a puzzling miracle, Master Tabary, and ungenerous of the saint to show me my loyal follower in prison in Burgundy and in peril of death. Pah, for such miracles! I want my brave and loyal follower near my person, where he can make himself useful."

A COACH FOR TRAVELING.

"And that," said Master Tabary, nodding his head, "with the saint's aid, my plan will bring to pass."

The great company sat at meat in the refectory hall, the King and the Abbot side by side beneath the tall window in the end wall, with the knights and some favored members of the royal household below them. It was a fine room, its ceiling high and supported on a series of tall arches laid flat against the long side-wall. The sun poured a welcome light through many windows, and the gray stone walls softened it to a glowing twilight. By the monastery rules the monks must eat without speaking, and the knights were content to obey that rule, since from the oratory at the far end of the long hall there always rose the chant of a reader intoning the gracious words of some Latin book of devotion. Reverently the knights and monks listened through their meals. But since a king had done them the honor of a visit, this day the rule of silence was broken, and from the oratory came the sound of music—a harp, three viols, two flutes, a lute, and the organ from the monks' hall, which had been carried up there for the day. There were some gay songs and marches, but since they were monks who played, hymns and chants as well.

The music sounded doubly fine under the great arched roof, but the King was not pleased. The meal seemed to him hours long. He talked with the Abbot, but he was not gay. He was studying the company assembled. Each single man, knight, monk, soldier, came under his gaze, and he was unsatisfied, restless. Somewhere among the pilgrims in the guest house Margot Dieudonné was waiting for his promise to rescue her son, and he could not promise, for he had no one to send.

THE MONKS PLAYED ON THE ORGAN.

The great bell of the abbey rang out five strokes. The King rose suddenly, and the Abbot jumped hastily to his feet. When a king decides to linger no more over his meal, no one else dares continue to eat. The whole company sprang up after the Abbot. It had been a magnificent feast, and they had expected the King to speak to them, but he walked out of the hall without a word. After him went the Abbot and the members of the royal household. The monks and knights of the Abbey sat down again, to talk, at least, for they had eaten to repletion.

"The tide is out, is it not?" asked the King.

"Yes, Sire, full out," answered the Abbot.

"For how long will it be safe to walk upon the sands?" asked the King, fingering his wide jeweled collar.

"A half-hour or more," answered the Abbot, wondering. "Does your Majesty wish to walk upon the sands?"

"Yes," said the King, "though I would it were possible to do so without climbing all these stairs again. So many stairs I have not mounted in one day since I toiled to the top of the Cathedral of Our Lady in Paris."

"Nor did you, then, Sire," answered the Abbot, smiling. "This mighty rock is almost twice as high as Notre Dame's highest spire."

"Nevertheless," said the King, testily, "I must go down those stairs, and when I have walked on the sands I will climb them all again, perforce, for here I sleep to-night. That tide—faster than a horse can gallop . . ." He smiled sourly. "Come, Master Tabary, call a man or two, enough for our dignity in public sight, and bring your pretty daughter also. We would not go dully, with no beauty· in our train."

Down the King started, the good Abbot beside him, grumbling a little. It seemed a stupid whim, to go down so many stairs for a dull promenade on the flat beach only to return again so soon to the rock—if he were not to be drowned in the swift inrush of the waters.

"Colette!" Master Tabary called. "And you, Marie, attend Mistress Colette—and Charles of Mont Vason, and Thomas of Le Puy. You will be enough. No danger threatens here. Ah, André, come, too, and bring your tablets. Some one of us may need a clerk to write a suddenly remembered note. Bring your dog, if so you can find him quickly. A good dog is worth five men-at-arms."

André flushed with pleasure at being called to attend the King so closely. "A moment only, to get the dog!" he cried, and rushed off excitedly, around a dozen corners, through two long corridors, and downward to the great mass of the guest building where he had left the animal tied, lest his great bulk frighten the gentle monks. As he drew near deep barks of welcome made a sick man lying in the corner shout out crossly that there should be a way to keep the creature silent. André untied him without answering the man in the corner, and together they ran out and back to the street of stairs by which the King and his party were already descending to the base of the tall rock. The dog bounded down, then turned back to André's side again, then down the long stairs

TO·GETHER·THEY·RAN·OUT·AND·BACK·TO·THE·STREET·OF·STAIRS

and back a hundred times before at last they came up with
the King's party. Then André called the beast to his side to
walk in seemly fashion at the rear of the small procession.

Proudly the young man walked there. It was the first time
such an honor had been done him, and it made him feel that
at last fortune had turned for him. Colette's father had
called him. Perhaps that meant that Colette's father had
taken notice of him, singled him out from the crowd of young
clerks, and thought him somehow more worthy of notice
than they. And then he shrugged his shoulders and told himself sternly to hold no such absurd thoughts. Life for him
must be a matter of keeping records with what humility he
could muster. Great deeds and the King's notice were for
men more deserving of favors. He, in humble fashion, must
do the simple things from day to day required of him, and
keep his dreams to himself or at most write them on paper.
That was the life of a clerk.

They emerged from the high wall of the mount by a small
postern door, set deep under the protection of a tower. "A
door that in time of danger is walled up as solid as the battlements," explained the Abbot. "In peaceful times like these
we open it for convenience."

A half-dozen men were busy on the sands, gathering the
tiny jumping fish known as white bait, which the tide had
left behind. A hundred would make a modest meal for a
man, but delicious enough for a king. Still, they were considered humble fare, and the King had been fed on wild-boar
meat, and goose wings, with a full red wine to wash them

down. There had been sweet cakes too, and a roasted pea-
cock, and venison pasty, and wild birds with a spiced sauce.
Pears and apples and grapes had been left in their carven
silver dish to grace the table, but the King was ready to walk
upon the sands before he had time to touch them. André,
having been brought up far from the sea, was amazed by the
millions of tiny fishes that jumped like live silver in the sunlight. He paid scant heed to them, however. He watched
Colette and the King, and kept his dog quiet with his hand
on the animal's collar. The King and Colette were walking
side by side, she demurely listening, as becomes a simple
maid whose lord has chosen to honor her with his notice.

It was the first time that André had seen her so singled
out, and except that the Abbot walked on her other side, he
would have made himself ill with wondering what the King
might be saying. Watching carefully, he decided that it was
not of much importance. The King walked slowly, his head
held a little to the left, and when he spoke it seemed to be in
short speeches, and without smiling. The gatherers of the
white bait turned, one by one, and made their way back
toward the fortress, but the King went on. The Abbot spoke
to him, motioning toward the fishermen, and when the King
had answered, the Abbot and the knights with him turned to
leave their sovereign and Colette and her father staring out
toward the sea. André, the youngest and humblest of the
company, was last. He stopped when they turned, and drew
aside, to take his place at the end of the procession again.
One of the knights spoke to him. "Follow," he said, "his

"FOLLOW," HE SAID, "HIS MAJESTY WOULD STAND ALONE FOR A FEW

MOMENTS TO CONTEMPLATE THE BEAUTIES OF THE COAST."

Majesty would stand alone for a few moments to contemplate the beauties of the coast."

Obediently André turned and walked with them half a hundred feet. He would have said it was not safe if he had had any one to say it to, but he was of such a humble station that not one of the knights ever spoke to him except to give an order, or to make a gracious, patronizing comment on some unimportant subject like the weather.

The dog sat down to wait, and then stood up again suddenly. The sands were cold and damp. And then Colette and her father left the King quite alone, staring out at the sea. England lay over there, well out of sight. André wondered if Louis were considering a second French conquest of that enemy island. Then, his Majesty seemed to have finished his staring. He turned quickly and rejoined Colette and her father, and presently the three were back among the little company of the escort, the Abbot restless with fear of the tide, the King walking jerkily and casting an occasional glance backward, as though measuring the distance to the wall of water that would presently advance across the flat expanse of sand. They had all seen it come in soon after reaching the mount, and had shuddered at its relentless rush. André looked backward now, and saw again the white line of surf in the distance. The King saw it also, and suddenly spoke.

"My collar!" he said. "I have dropped my jeweled collar. I had it back where I stood alone. Some one must go back. Master Tabary, choose one to go back."

"I will go," said the Abbot. "It is a dangerous errand, but surely the waters would not drown the Abbot of St. Michael's Mount."

Voices were raised in protest at the Abbot's so risking himself, but they stopped again as André and his dog ran back across the sands. Colette cried out, but her father silenced her.

"He has long legs and good lungs," he said, "and he was the youngest and humblest here. It was his duty to go, and he was brave enough and loyal enough to go freely without being bid."

The white line of surf was sharper, nearer, now. André knew that he could reach the spot where the King had stood before it reached him. He was sure of that. But could he return? Faster than a horse can gallop!

The dog raced ahead of him, then turned and bounded back, and raced on again before him as he ran down across the white hard, flat sands, toward the spot where the footsteps ended in their path toward the advancing sea. It was farther than he thought. His breath began to come shorter, and the dog settled down to run steadily at his side. The line of surf drew nearer. It drew nearer still with a threatening swiftness. There was a gleam of bright color on the sand, and André raced for it. There, just a little ahead, was the edge of dark water. It made a rushing sound, a sucking sound, as it advanced. A menacing white and green line, uneven, advancing and retreating, swirling, surprisingly high above the level of the beach. Faster than a horse can gallop! It was almost upon him. Only a few dozen feet . . . and he could not run as fast as a horse could gallop. Not for long. At least, he never had. And the dark high stone wall that offered haven to him was so far away.

He had the collar now. The King's collar, inherited from his father, and his father—perhaps even from the great St. Louis for whom this Louis was named. A very precious collar. He clutched it securely in his hand. What if he should be drowned? He had heard that bodies drowned in the sea, even though carried out, came back again at another point along the coast. The collar must not be lost. It was as cold and hard as the King's voice, but a symbol of his royalty, almost like his crown. The dog was running close now, seeming to know that danger threatened. André increased his speed a little. The surf was just behind him. Ahead, a slight figure in a blue cloak was standing on the wall, with a group around it. Colette—Colette in the cloak that made her look like a figure of Our Lady! The King's party was safe from the sea's rush. The thought helped him to run faster. Colette was waiting for him.

And then a long, licking wave washed his feet. Foaming whitely, it rushed up the beach for a long distance beyond him, and softened the sand so that his footsteps sank into the once hard surface. He would have fallen if he had not slowed his speed. The wave receded. It was a very thin, flat, wide wave, but it ran swiftly up the beach and was followed very quickly by a second, deeper and stronger. André felt it strike against his ankles and rush past them, then felt its strong pull as it ran back. Behind that came, fast and quick, wave after wave, each deeper than the last, and suddenly one threw him from his feet into a surging torrent. He tried to swim, but the current was so strong that he was borne forward in spite of himself toward the walls of the mount, but helplessly, at the mercy of the sea. Against its inevitable surge he could do little but keep himself afloat. Beside him swam the dog, seeming to have less difficulty than his master in the strong current. They were almost under the walls. Some one shouted and threw a rope. It was washed beyond him, and then he was carried out again, away from the rock, and then back, and so—forward and back—he and the dog struggled, keeping as near to each other as they could.

Water rushed across André's face, water in his eyes, in his nose. So fierce was the driving surf that he knew his strength was going. He had no more breath, the waves were too strong, his arms refused to answer his desperate need, and he felt himself sinking, rolling over and over in a sea that was no longer dark-green, but black as night, black as the darkness of dreams, and full of the agony of trying to breathe where there was no air, only solid water all around.

It was the dog who saved him. As he sank, the great animal came close to him and André, feeling his bulk, found his leather collar, and held fast to it, desperately. The dog fought the sea by instinct, taking advantage of the forward surge of the waves, and gained ground now in spite of his burden. They were again close under the rock, and two native men, strong swimmers, flung themselves into the flood, and dragged the unconscious boy and the now exhausted dog to safety. The King stood looking down at them. Colette dropped to her knees, weeping and wringing her hands.

"He is dead!" she cried. "Oh, St. Michael, have mercy, he is dead!"

But he was not dead. His eyes opened for an instant, then closed again, weakly.

"Here is your second brave and loyal man, Sire," said Master Tabary. "The saint has been generous. He has shown you two."

"Aye," said the King, indifferently, "two. One in prison and one a bungler. If this one lives I will reward him by sending him to Burgundy to rescue the other, but he has come back without the collar. What is such a one? He will fail again in Burgundy. Bravery and loyalty are useless things if they do not lead to accomplishment. He has failed." Louis turned away.

A monk skillful with medicines had run down from the abbey, and now he leaned over André. He opened his shirt with quick fingers to feel his heart. There against his body lay the bright collar, stowed safely, though its rescuer might drown. With a cry Master Tabary snatched it from its resting-place, and held it toward the King.

"Now that," said his Majesty fervently, "is a different matter. Will he live, brother?" The hard voice was all eagerness.

The monk nodded. "In an hour he will be as well as ever,

your Majesty," he answered. "He needs but a few minutes' rest and air for his lungs."

To prove it André opened his eyes again, and smiled at Colette. The King came to stand over him.

"You shall enter my personal service," he announced, and André saw that his usually suspicious eyes were kindly now. "This evening you start on a mission of importance, and I will grant, as still further reward, whatever request you may make—in reason, of course."

"Then," cried André, excitedly, "your Majesty—is it within reason to ask—the accolade—before I leave?"

"The accolade?" King Louis laughed. "He asks the accolade! The brave and loyal must be a knight! Knighthood is reserved for those of noble birth. Still, I am glad you did not ask for gold. Knighthood is cheaper. A knight should be brave and loyal and you are both. This is a day of miracles, and when the saint finds me two loyal brave men where I had hoped for no more than one—for they are scarce, Master Tabary, scarce indeed—aye, then on this day the King of France too can work a miracle, and recognize him of noble birth that lives nobly. Perhaps that is no miracle, but there are those who think it so. If you have strength yet, arise, Sir —André, is it not? Knight you are from this moment forth. Master Tabary, see that he departs as soon as may be on my mission, and takes that fine dog with him. I leave this young miracle in your hands, and will receive him again when he brings me back from the prison of Burgundy my second miracle, Philip, good Margot's son."

The great bell of the Abbey Church clanged out the hour. Six strokes.

"St. Michael has answered all our prayers," said Colette. "Come, André, my now noble knight, let us give thanks to St. Michael of the Mount."

And you, if you also make pilgrimage to the mount, can hear that bell to-day, and see the great church and the Merveille, and watch the rushing tide as it sweeps madly across the white sands where André once risked his life for loyalty to grim King Louis.

THE ARMS OF THE ABBEY.

A City in the Sea

The battlements of Mont Saint-Michel rise straight and marvelously tall from the flat sands of the coast, and the tide rushes in with the same thunderous sweep that it did when André was nearly drowned in it. It is exciting to watch even if every one is safely behind the battlements of the mount.

At first glimpse the rock looks as though it had been carelessly thrown on the wide beach by some giant hand. There is a legend that it was the top of a mountain in the ancient land of Ys. And so it may have been, for the legend relates how that fabled land sank beneath the ocean, and of it only this narrow rocky peak remained. However that may be, there are no other portions of Ys anywhere at all, so it is hard to prove, though pleasant to think about.

MONT · SAINT~MICHEL · TO~DAY

King Louis had to wait for the tides when he went on horseback to the mount, but you can drive there in a car, no matter how high the tide may be, for there is now a wide causeway that connects the island with the mainland. It is a surprisingly long drive, and there is nothing at all between you and the battlements of the mount. You will have time to view each detail from a distance, and then nearer . . . and nearer. First, there are the ancient battlements. Above them is a tiny village of clustering houses, all much newer than the time of Louis the King. They are close together, because the rock is so steep that all the streets are streets of stairs, and there is little room for building. Above the houses are the lower portions of the monastery, then the Merveille, and to crown the whole, the tall spire of the great church, with a new and shining figure of St. Michael brandishing his sword high in the air.

It is an enormous pile, laid stone upon stone by monks and pilgrims through a thousand years, in honor of Michael the Archangel, commander of the hosts of Heaven. He was a most appropriate patron for the mount, since it has been from the first as much fortress as abbey or place of pilgrimage. Far more than at Carcassonne or Avignon, its ancient buildings are intact, with all their heavy walls and narrow window-nooks, their half-hidden corners and great spaces, one above the other, rising out of the sea like a fairy-tale city. Up and up and up you climb, and then up again, an unbelievable number of stairs, from the battlemented walls to the high glory of the ancient church.

Great soldiers have always loved the fortress abbey, and many of the most famous have made pilgrimage to it. Duke William of Normandy went many times, and set out from the neighboring coasts to conquer England. The towers of the church must have been a landmark for steering part of his fleet. King Richard the Lion-Hearted, William's son, made pilgrimage also, as did Philip the Fair, who built the tower that still bears his name at the Villeneuve end of the bridge of St. Benezet.

Charles, the father of Louis XI, also made pilgrimage to the mount in the dark days before he was crowned king, when the English overran France. He prayed there to St. Michael, the soldier-archangel, and the saint answered by appearing to Joan of Arc, so the legend runs, and guiding her to drive back the English. Louis must have thought of that aid to his father as he made his prayer in gratitude and hope of further favors for himself and for his people.

As he prayed to St. Michael he must have thought, also, as you will, of all the long lines of pilgrims who have made the journey to the mount, through more than two thousand years. The earliest of them were not Christian, for the mount was a holy place in the days of the Druids, the priests of Gaul before the Romans came. They called it Mount Belenus, in honor of their god of the sun, and the altar was tended by priestesses who spent their lives praying for the safety of the seamen among the treacherous tides of the coast.

The Romans came next, called the place Mount Jupiter, and raised an altar to that god. The early Christians called it "Tumba," which means "a high place." Hermits lived there then. It was not until a little before Pepin entered Carcassonne that it became Mont Saint-Michel.

A bishop named Aubert had a vision of St. Michael, and the archangel asked the good bishop to build a church on the rock. Of course he did. That church is said to have been round, and to have provided living-space for a hundred people. Aubert chose as its site the exact summit of the rock. Nothing lower would be good enough for the archangel's own church, but there were difficulties. The rock was so sharp and high that there was no place for workmen to stand. The peak had to be leveled, and there seemed no way to do it, so after the manner of the Middle Ages the good bishop prayed for a miracle, and one was granted. He lifted up a small child and placed its foot upon the highest point of the rock, and immediately the point broke off and rolled down into the sea, leaving a smooth space just large enough for the chapel, and bearing on its surface the imprint of a child's foot for proof of the miracle through the centuries to come.

No one knows exactly where that church was, and during the years the rock has been built upon so often that the structures rose higher and higher, until the abbey has come to be called the "Marvel." The builders kept their eyes on the highest point, and were so busy looking upward that they forgot entirely what was under the stones they laid. And then, one day, only a short while ago, a discovery was made.

EACH·POOR·PILGRIM·WHO·WALKED·SLOWLY·TO·THE·MOUNT·LEFT·AN·OFFERING

A whole church had been walled up under the left platform, and forgotten! A staircase was found, leading downward, and silent and lonely under the mass of buildings above, there was the church. It was not Bishop Aubert's church, but one built after his, perhaps above his. You can see it if you go to the mount. They call it the Church of Our Lady Underground. It was built a few years after Pepin marched into Carcassonne, and probably walled up by Abbot Guillaume d'Estouteville.

When Duke William of Normandy set sail for England, in 1066, there was a still newer church, very large and handsome, with enormously heavy walls and strong towers. Part of that building you can see, for it forms the center of the present high church, under the St. Michael on the spire. It was such a heavy mass that the rock on which it was supported crumbled under the weight. There were two towers at the entrance, and a wide choir at the opposite end. First one tower fell, and then in 1421 the choir collapsed and, like the top of the mountain in Bishop Aubert's miracle, went rolling down into the sea. But this was not a miracle—it was a calamity.

That same war with England to which Jehanne's father was called was still being fought—it lasted for a hundred years—and there was no chance or money to do anything about a crumbling church. Too many other things were happening. The monks prayed, the pilgrims sorrowed, the English attacked and were repulsed. At last the great day came when Joan of Arc led the French army to victory, and

after some years more Louis XI became king. There was
peace along the coast at last, and he arranged that a very
rich friend of his, Guillaume d'Estouteville, should become
Abbot of Mont Saint-Michel. Guillaume—that is "William"
in English—was delighted, as Louis knew he would be. He

SOLDIER WINDING A CROSSBOW.

had always loved the mount, and immediately began to repair
the ruined buildings at his own cost. He built a new tower
and the lovely choir with tall windows full of glowing
colored glass, and then invited his royal friend to see what
he had done. The King who had made Guillaume Abbot in
the hope that he would rebuild the church, gladly and gratefully made the journey, as we have read in the story "Acco-

lade." So little has been changed since that when you go there you can know that you are seeing just what King Louis and André and Colette saw.

You can go through the same door they went through, at the end of the church, and enter a dismal room that was used as a dormitory by the monks. They were not supposed to concern their minds with bodily comforts, but they must have enjoyed the hours they spent in the cool shade of the cloister near-by, or in the warm sunshine of the garden in its center. It is one of the loveliest cloisters in the world. A double row of slender carved columns surrounds the court, to form a covered gallery, roofed in colored tiles of orange and blue. It was designed for the pleasure of the monks at their meditations, a place where they could go in quiet to breathe the salt air of the sea, away from the thronging crowds of pilgrims.

When you have wandered long enough in the cloister, you will want, as King Louis did, to return to the great platform before the church, and stare out at the view for miles around. Just below are small gabled houses with tiny terraced gardens, the walls, the sands—and beyond them, to one side, across the sea, you know that England lies, to the other, green and fair in its nearness, the mainland of France.

To King Louis that France of his was already a nation, not a mere stretch of country over whose quarrelsome counts and barons and dukes he was lord. It was his dream to unite all of the old Roman province of Gaul under the crown of

THE NEW CHOIR WITH TALL WINDOWS OF COLORED GLASS.

France, and to that end he had carried before him, in battle and on the most solemn occasions, a special banner, called the "oriflamme"—the "golden flame"—which has been drawn here for you to see. It was a sacred flag, not of the royal house, but of St. Denis, the patron saint of Paris. People thought it such a holy thing that they knelt in the dust of the streets as it was carried past them.

THE ORIFLAMME.

Our national flag, and that of France to-day, are made thousands of times over in the same patterns, and remain the symbols of nationality even if sold on a street corner. It is the design to which men tip their hats as their flag is carried in a parade. But King Louis' oriflamme was a single piece of red silk, made holy by being blessed by the monks of

St. Denis. Copied, it would have been a forgery, like a counterfeit banknote. Only that one piece of silk was of any consequence, though when it wore out it could be replaced, and the new flag blessed again. Originally it had belonged to the Monastery of St. Denis in Paris. The Kings of France called themselves "Defenders of St. Denis," and so won the right to carry the oriflamme of France's glory. It was embroidered in gold and hung from a golden bar, and its points represented the points of flames.

Poor King Louis needed something beautiful like the oriflamme, for there was certainly nothing very glamorous about him. He had a thin face and a long nose and dressed shabbily in dark clothes, always a little out of style—as an example, because he hated extravagance in dress. Perhaps he was right, for the people of his day were very fond indeed of beautiful clothes, and sewed them over with jewels and thread of real gold. The women wore immensely tall headdresses with flowing veils. Luckily ceilings were made high enough in those days so that they did not have to go about on their knees.

King Louis's own hat was a low affair, and he is famous for hanging a row of little leaden images of saints around its brim. It is really one of the least remarkable things he ever did, for such images were very much the fashion then. The streets and roads were full of robbers, and the help of the saints was asked on journeys, especially that of St. Christopher and St. Nicholas, who are both patrons of travelers. Hanging

PEOPLE WORE BEAUTIFUL CLOTHES.

their images on your hat was supposed to enlist their interest in your trip. But there were not many people brave enough, or with faith enough, to go unarmed and trust to the saints to protect them. Every knight carried a sword, and every one else a dagger or at least a stout stick.

Guns were not yet light or dependable enough to be used by robbers or for travelers' protection, so hold-ups were at the point of a dagger, or perhaps the robber used a club first, and did his robbing quietly while his victim lay unconscious. But though guns were still cumbersome, uncertain things, armorers went on experimenting with the tricky and dangerous *batons à feu*, until at last—but it is a long story, how they grew into modern firearms. The people of the fif-

A DANGEROUS *BATON A FEU.*

teenth century were not greatly concerned with them. Crossbows were the most formidable battle weapons of that day.
They shot heavy arrows a long distance, so effectively that
they could pierce through armor. They were accurate, too,
which was a great deal more than could be said of the
clumsy "fire-sticks." Very probably not a single firearm
went with King Louis to Mont Saint-Michel. But there must
have been crossbows, swords in plenty, and lances with gay
pennons waving from their tips, and the knights were re-
splendent in their shining armor.

They were all hungry by the time they arrived at the top
of the mount, and no doubt the first thing Abbot Guillaume
thought of when his royal guest arrived was food for his
entertainment. Cooking had grown to be a much more delicate matter than it was in Pepin's day, or even in Pope

Clement's time. The millers had learned to refine flour so that bread could be made lighter and whiter. The cooks were busy inventing new dishes, sweet cakes, meat pies, and sauces to add flavor to their boiled meats. Meals were served in numerous courses, after the old Roman fashion. At Abbot Guillaume's table no doubt all the honored guests had forks for their meats, not merely for fruits. Between courses they laid them on rests, to wait for the next opportunity to use them. The more elaborate food became, the more necessary forks seemed. A plain, almost dry bit of meat could be eaten satisfactorily with the fingers, but a dripping concoction of mushrooms and herb-flavored sauce was not so easy to manage without help.

The honored guest still sat "back to the fire and stomach to the table," and of course there was a fireplace in every important room of the abbey. Abbot Guillaume saw to it that they were in the new fashion, deep and wide like caves, so that they would burn immense logs. Sometimes they were so large that they had seats under the hood, and people could sit there to read or chat and still be far enough from the flame to be in no danger of scorching.

At that time firelight was almost as good as any other artificial light. Only one little invention made lighting better than it had been for a thousand years past. Open lamps spill their oil if they are tipped. That made the lighting of wagons and ships dangerous because of fire. Early in the fifteenth century some one arranged a way to hang the oil cups of

OF COURSE THERE WAS A FIREPLACE IN EVERY
IMPORTANT ROOM OF THE ABBEY.

lamps in the center of swinging circles of metal, so that the flame would always remain upright, no matter how roughly

A CANDLESTICK.

a ship or a wagon might roll about. The same useful invention kept the hot charcoal in hand warmers from tumbling out, and people carried them gratefully on drives and to the huge, cold churches. They were pretty toys, and extremely practical as well. King Louis and his courtiers must have had one or two of the swinging lamps and several of the hand warmers on the trip to Mont Saint-Michel, for they could not have been too expensive even for the household of a poor king who set an example of thriftiness to his people.

You have read in the story of "Accolade" how Abbot Guillaume ordered music to play for the king during dinner.

People have always liked to hear music with their meals, and then no less than now they liked dancing with their music. The dancers hung themselves with bells, like the girl in the Mother Goose rhyme,

A DANCER.

"With bells on her fingers,
And rings on her toes,
She shall have music
Wherever she goes!"

She was a dancer, of course. The jesters, or fools, whose business it was to amuse people in castles and courts, took up the idea, jingled gayly at every movement, and pointed their jokes with a fine tintinnabulation.

But of course all that did not happen at Mont Saint-Michel, for the mount was a holy place, and except for sacred music there was little thought of entertainment there. The monks could play various instruments, and during

A HAND ORGAN.

a king's visit they might divert a royal guest at dinner, but the usual practice during meals was the reading aloud of some religious book. The gallery in which the musicians played was the place from which the reading was done, and you can still climb up to it, if you wish, high in the wall of the refectory hall.

The books from which the reading was done were hand-copied ones, but it is very probable that if Colette had asked

the Abbot Guillaume to show her his library, he would have
brought out from one of the chests where he kept his volumes
a really remarkable novelty—a printed book! Colette could
not have seen many of them, and she would have been inter-

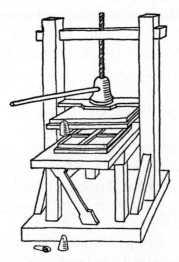

THE GUTENBERG PRESS.

ested, though it would have been rather clumsily made, and
not nearly so handsome as the hand-written ones. She would
probably have said, "Oh, yes, that German invention! Ugly,
isn't it? I wonder if they will ever make anything of printing?"

The Abbot Guillaume would have thought not, it was such
a laborious process. Each type letter cut by hand, and the
printing done slowly page by page. Printing from type was

actually invented by a German named Johannes Gutenberg about the year 1450, but as the Abbot noted, making the type was such a slow process that in the time of Louis's visit to Mont Saint-Michel it was still quite unimportant, and its inventor had gone bankrupt.

The world and France have changed a great deal since the turbulent days of King Louis, but Mont Saint-Michel is almost as it was. You can step back through its gateway five hundred years, or a thousand years, if you wish. You can stand on the stones on which King Louis stood, and look at the great choir the Abbot Guillaume showed him, or you can go down into the Church of Our Lady Underground, and put your hand on walls that were old when another Guillaume, he of Normandy, whom we call William the Conqueror, prayed to the Archangel Michael of the mount. You can watch the tides come in with a rush, and feel yourself very close indeed to the vanished ages when Euric and Pepin, Jehanne and Pope Clement, and André and Colette and King Louis breathed the bright air of the ancient land that we call France.

How to pronounce the foreign words and names.

Accolade—ăk'ŏ-läd'

André—än'drā

Aubert—ō'bẹr

Avignon—ȧ'vē'nyÔN'

Barbican—bär'bĭ-căn

Baton à feu, or batons à feu—bȧ'tÔN'ä fû

Belenus—bĕ'lẹ'nŭs

Benezet—bĕn'ĕ-zĕt'

Boccaccio—bŏ-kä'chyō

Bourgeois—bōōr'zhwȧ'

Bourgeoise—bōōr'zhwȧz'

Carcassonne—kär'kä-sŏn'

Chevalier—shĕ-vȧ'lyā'

Clerc: Jehan le Clerc—zhän lû-clär'

Colette—kō'lĕt'

Dieudonné—dyŭ'dŏn-ā'

Euric—ûr'ĭk

Farandole—fȧr'äN-dōl'

Guillaume d'Estouteville—gē'yōm' dĕs'-tōōt'vē'

Gutenberg—gōō'tĕn-bĕrκ

Jehan—zhän

Jehanne—zhänn

Jongleur, or jongleurs—zhÔN'glûr'

Liege—lēj

Livrée, or livrées—lē'vrā'

Machicoulis—mä'shĭ-kōō'lē'

Margot—mär'gō'

Matteo Giovannetti—mät-tā'ō jō'vän-nĕt'tē

Mont Saint-Michel—mÔN' säN'-mē-shĕl'

Noël—nŏ-ĕl'

Oriflamme—ŏr'ĭ-flăm

Paesse—pä-ĕs

Pepin—pĕ'păN'

Petrarch—pä-trärk'

Provence—prŏ'väNs'

Régnier—rā'nyā'

Renaissance—rĕn'ĕ-säNs'

Rheims, Notre Dame, Amiens—răNs, nō'tr' dȧm', ȧ'myăN'

Saint: when combined with a French word—säN

Tabary—tăb'ä-rē'

Tumba—tŏŏm'bä

Vilain—vē-län'

Villeneuve—vēl'nûv'

Ys: the Land of Ys—ēss

169

BIBLIOGRAPHY

Carcassonne, in Mentor Magazine, November, 1928.

Viollet-le-Duc, Carcassonne.

Gibbon, Decline and Fall of the Roman Empire.

Foncin, Guide à la cité de Carcassonne.

Crois-Mayreville, Histoire du Comté, et de la Vicomté, de Carcassonne.

Fédie, Histoire de Carcassonne.

J. Poux, La cité de Carcassonne.

Guizot, Short History of France.

Encyclopædia Britannica, various articles.

London Archæological Journal, various articles.

Firebaugh, Inns of The Middle Ages.

R. T. Hamson, Medii Ævi Kalendarium.

Eileen Power, Mediæval People.

C. Bich, Le château et la vie de château.

Grande encyclopédie, various articles.

R. Rosières, Histoire de la société au moyen âge.

Gaston Paris, La légende de Pépin le Bref.

D'Allemagne, Histoire du lumière.

Lacroix, Les arts au moyen âge.

Lacroix, Mœurs et coutumes.

Viollet-le-Duc, Dictionnaire du mobilier français.

Esther Singleton, Dolls.

L. F. Salzmann, Mediæval Byways.

E. M. Tappan, In Feudal Times.

Collection des meilleurs notices relatif à l'histoire de France. Part 5,
Volume 8.

Litchfield, History of Furniture.

Robert Brun, Avignon au temps des papes.

A. S. Forrest, Tour Through Old Provence.

Henry Adams, Mont Saint Michel and Chartres.

Nuova enciclopedia italiana, "Giovanna di Napoli."

T. A. Cook, Old Provence.

Watson, Story of France.

Louis Blondel, Notice historique du Mont-Saint-Michel.

Thomas Okey, The Story of Avignon.

L. H. Labande, Le palais des papes et les monuments d'Avignon au
     XIVe siècle.

Joseph Breck and Meyric R. Rogers, The Pierpont Morgan Wing of
     The Metropolitan Museum of Art.

Étienne Dupont, Les légendes du Mont-Saint-Michel.

Edmond Haraucourt, Mediæval Manners Illustrated at the Cluny Museum.

Guides Joanne, Avignon et ses environs.

Jean Girou, Carcassonne, Its City, Its Crown.

Ch.-H. Besnard, Le Mont-Saint-Michel.